Society of Colonial Wars

History of the Society of Colonial Wars in the State of California

List of Officers and Members

Society of Colonial Wars

History of the Society of Colonial Wars in the State of California
List of Officers and Members

ISBN/EAN: 9783337154462

Printed in Europe, USA, Canada, Australia, Japan

Cover: Foto ©ninafisch / pixelio.de

More available books at **www.hansebooks.com**

HISTORY

OF THE

SOCIETY OF COLONIAL WARS

IN THE

STATE OF CALIFORNIA

LIST OF OFFICERS AND MEMBERS

PROCEEDINGS OF THE FIRST GENERAL COURT
AT LOS ANGELES, MARCH 7, 1896

Publication No. 1

LOS ANGELES
1896

CONTENTS.

	PAGE
Membership Roll	4
Officers	5–6
Historical Sketch of Organization	7–10
First General Court	11
Address of Governor	15–19
Address of John Randolph Haynes, M. D.	21–27
Address of Frank Clarke Prescott	29–34
Address of Major William Anthony Elderkin, U.S.A.	35–38
Address of George Jules Denis	38
Memoriam, Harry Woodville Latham	39–40
List of Members, showing their descent from ancestors who performed services in Colonial Wars	41–50

MEMBERSHIP ROLL.

BREWER, REV. WILLIAM AUGUSTUS, Clergyman, - San Mateo.
COLLINS, HOLDRIDGE OZRO, Lawyer, - - - - Los Angeles.
COLTON, PROF. ALLEN LYSANDER, Astronomer, Lick Observatory.
DENIS, GEORGE JULES, United States District Attorney, - Los Angeles.
ELDERKIN, LIEUT.-COL. WILLIAM ANTHONY, U.S.A., Chicago, Ill.
FENNER, CHARLES PUTNAM, Journalist, - - - - Los Angeles.
FLINT, FRANK PUTNAM, Lawyer, - - - - - Los Angeles.
FLINT, MOTLEY HEWES, Postoffice Inspector, - - - Los Angeles.
HARDEN, EDWARD THOMAS, Electrician, - - - Los Angeles.
HAYNES, JOHN RANDOLPH, M. D., Physician, - - Los Angeles.
HOLDEN, PROF. EDWARD SINGLETON, Astronomer, Lick Observatory.
LEE, BRADNER WELLS, Lawyer, - - - - Los Angeles.
MERWIN, REV. ALEXANDER MOSS, Clergyman, - Pasadena, Cal.
McKINSTRY, HON. ELISHA WILLIAMS,
    Ex-Justice Supreme Court, Lawyer, San Francisco.
NICHOLS, HENRY ATHERTON, Rancher, - - - - Redlands.
NICHOLS, WILLARD ATHERTON, Rancher, - - - Redlands.
PAYSON, CAPT. ALBERT HENRY, Capitalist, - - San Mateo.
PRESCOTT, FRANK CLARKE, Lawyer, - - - - Redlands.
ROSS, HON. ERSKINE MAYO, United States Circuit Judge, Los Angeles.
THOM, HON. CAMERON ERSKINE, Lawyer, ex-Mayor, - Los Angeles.
THORPE, ANDREW ROANE, Dentist, - - - - Los Angeles.
THORPE, SPENCER ROANE, Rancher, - - - - Los Angeles.

OFFICERS 1896.

Governor,
HOLDRIDGE OZRO COLLINS,
Los Angeles.

Deputy Governor,
HON. ERSKINE MAYO ROSS.

Lieutenant Governor,
LIEUT.-COL. WILLIAM ANTHONY ELDERKIN, U. S. A.

Secretary,
CHARLES PUTNAM FENNER,
930 S. Flower St., Los Angeles.

Treasurer,
FRANK PUTNAM FLINT.
First and Spring Sts., Los Angeles

Registrar,
EDWARD THOMAS HARDEN.

Historian,
BRADNER WELLS LEE.

Chancellor,
GEORGE JULES DENIS.

Surgeon,
JOHN RANDOLPH HAYNES, M. D.

Chaplain,
REV. ALEXANDER MOSS MERWIN.

Gentlemen of the Council.
SPENCER ROANE THORPE, *Chairman.*
REV. WILLIAM AUGUSTUS BREWER,
WILLARD ATHERTON NICHOLS,
CHARLES PUTNAM FENNER,
MOTLEY HEWES FLINT,
HON. CAMERON ERSKINE THOM,
HENRY ATHERTON NICHOLS,
ANDREW ROANE THORPE,
FRANK CLARKE PRESCOTT.

Committee on Membership.

BRADNER WELLS LEE, *Chairman.*
GEORGE JULES DENIS, *Secretary.*
FRANK PUTNAM FLINT,
JOHN RANDOLPH HAYNES, M. D.
SPENCER ROANE THORPE.

Committee on Historical Documents.

BRADNER WELLS LEE, *Chairman ex-officio.*
JOHN RANDOLPH HAYNES, M. D.
PROF. EDWARD SINGLETON HOLDEN,
REV. ALEXANDER MOSS MERWIN.

Delegates to the General Society.

HON. ELISHA WILLIAMS MCKINSTRY,
PROF. EDWARD SINGLETON HOLDEN,
CAPT. ALBERT HENRY PAYSON,
FRANK CLARKE PRESCOTT,
HOLDRIDGE OZRO COLLINS.

Alternates.

PROF. ALLEN LYSANDER COLTON,
MOTLEY HEWES FLINT,
HON. CAMERON ERSKINE THOM,
EDWARD THOMAS HARDEN,
HENRY ATHERTON NICHOLS.

Committee on Entertainment.

FRANK PUTNAM FLINT,
GEORGE JULES DENIS,
CHARLES PUTNAM FENNER,
JOHN RANDOLPH HAYNES, M. D.
FRANK CLARKE PRESCOTT.

Deputy Governor General.

SPENCER ROANE THORPE.

HISTORY OF THE CALIFORNIA SOCIETY.

ON THE fourteenth day of May, 1895, at a Council General of the Society of Colonial Wars, held at Baltimore, Maryland, Holdridge Ozro Collins, residing at Los Angeles, California, a member of the New York Society, was elected State Secretary for California.

On Saturday, the thirtieth day of November, 1895, the following named gentlemen, upon the invitation of Holdridge Ozro Collins and George Jules Denis, assembled in the office of the United States District Attorney for the Southern District of California, at the United States Government building, Los Angeles, California, for the purpose of discussing the feasibility of organizing a Society of Colonial Wars in the State of California, with its headquarters at Los Angeles, viz: Holdridge Ozro Collins, a member of the New York Society of Colonial Wars, Secretary for the State of California, George Jules Denis, United States District Attorney, a member of the New York Society of Colonial Wars, Major William Anthony Elderkin, U. S. A., Charles Putnam Fenner, Frank Putnam Flint, Motley Hughes Flint, John Randolph Haynes, M. D., Edward Thomas Harden, Bradner Wells Lee, the Rev. Alexander Moss Merwin, Willard Atherton Nichols, Hon. Erskine Mayo Ross, Judge of the United States Circuit Court, Ninth Circuit, Andrew Roane Thorpe, and Spencer Roane Thorpe.

The following named gentlemen were invited to be present at the said meeting, but being unable to attend, they were represented by certain of the foregoing named gentlemen who were present; viz., the Rev. William Augustus Brewer, Harry Woodville Latham, Henry Atherton Nichols, Josiah Alonzo Osgood, Hon. Cameron Erskine Thom, ex-Mayor of Los Angeles.

The meeting was called to order by Mr. Collins, whereupon Hon. Erskine Mayo Ross was selected as Chairman, and Charles Putnam Fenner as Secretary. Mr. Collins thereupon stated the object of the meeting, in a thoughtful and well considered address, and after a general discussion of the subject, resolutions were adopted that the gentlemen present at the meeting organize themselves into a Society of Colonial Wars in the State of California, subject to approval and confirmation by the General Society, and also that they accept as the elegibility qualification for membership, Article II of the Constitution of the General Society, and that they adopt for their temporary government so much of the Constitution and By-laws of the Society of Colonial Wars in the State of New York as might be applicable to the State of California.

The following officers were thereupon chosen: Governor, Holdridge Ozro Collins; Deputy Governor, Hon. Erskine Mayo Ross; Lieutenant Governor, Major William Anthony Elderkin, U. S. A.; Secretary, Harry Woodville Latham; Treasurer, Frank Putnam Flint; Registrar, Edward Thomas Harden; Historian, Bradner Wells Lee; Chancellor, George Jules Denis; Surgeon, John Randolph Haynes, M. D.; Chaplain, the Rev. Alexander Moss Merwin; Gentlemen of the Council, Spencer Roane Thorpe, Chairman, the Rev. William Augustus Brewer, Willard Atherton Nichols, Charles Putnam Fenner, Josiah Alonzo Osgood, Motley Hughes Flint, Hon. Cameron Erskine Thom, Henry Atherton Nichols, Andrew Roane Thorpe.

A petition to the General Society which had theretofore been prepared, was signed by all the gentlemen present and represented at this meeting, praying for a charter to the Society of Colonial Wars in the State of California. On the

10th day of December, 1895, the petition for a charter was mailed to the Secretary-General of the General Society of Colonial Wars. On December 19, 1895, the petition for the charter was granted by the General Council of Colonial Wars, and the official notification thereof was received by the Governor of this Society on Christmas morning, December 25, 1895.

On the 7th day of March, 1896, the First General Court of the Society of Colonial Wars in the State of California was held, followed by a banquet, in pursuance of a proclamation issued by the Governor, which was as follows:

From
H. O. COLLINS,
Los Angeles.

For Y^e hande of ye Moste Worshyppefulle

In ye Goodlie Cittie of

Situate in ye Pleasaunt Province of

These.

Postmanne,
Ride haste, post-haste with speede,
for thy lyffe, for thy lyffe, for thy lyffe.

Society of Colonial Wars
in the
State of California.

By Ye
Governor,
A Proclamation:

Ye First General Court of ye Society of Colonial Wars in ye Commonwealth of California will be convened atte ye hour of Seven, in ye evening of March 7, 1896, atte yᵉ Tavern of Jeremiah Illich on Third street in yᵉ Goodlie Cittie of Los Angeles. After yᵉ Enactment of such Laws as yᵉ Council recommend or yᵉ members propose, yᵉ General Court will Adjourn to partake of a Refreshment of Clams, Succotash, yᵉ Delectable Porke and Beanes, Pumpkin-pie, Chestnuts, Apples and Cider, to be served by yᵉ landlord at yᵉ ridiculous charge of $2.50.

Ye Committee of Arrangements request that You will inform yᵐ Promptly by yᵉ enclosed Card if You will attend.

Ye Treasurer will refuse to draw his Warrant for yᵉ Pay and mileage of all Absent Members.

Yᵉ INSIGNIA will be worn.

Dated yᵉ Twenty-Seventh day of February, A. D., 1896.

Holdridge Ozro Collins,

Governor.

By yᵉ Governor,
HARRY WOODVILLE LATHAM,
Secretary.

SOCIETY OF COLONIAL WARS,
FIRST GENERAL COURT
IN THE STATE OF CALIFORNIA.

ON THE 7th day of March, 1896, at the banquet hall of the restaurant of Jerry Illich, in the city of Los Angeles, the members of the Society met, pursuant to proclamation. The following were present: Holdridge Ozro Collins, George Jules Denis, Charles Putnam Fenner, Frank Putnam Flint, Motley Hughes Flint, Edward Thomas Harden, Harry Woodville Latham, Bradner Wells Lee, Frank Clarke Prescott, Hon. Cameron Erskine Thom, Spencer Roane Thorpe, Hon. Erskine Mayo Ross, Major William Anthony Elderkin, U. S. A., and John Randolph Haynes, M. D.

The meeting was called to order for the transaction of the business of the Society. The record of the original organization of the Society was then read and approved. The resignation of Josiah Alonzo Osgood as a member of the Council and Society was received and accepted. Frank Clarke Prescott was thereupon elected as a member of the Council to fill the vacancy created by the resignation of Josiah Alonzo Osgood. By-laws for the government of the Society, which had been previously prepared, were thereupon discussed, and finally adopted. Prof. Edward Singleton Holden and Bradner Wells Lee were appointed a committee to act with the Governor of the Society in the selection of a seal. A motion to incorporate the Society under the laws of the State of California was made, and after discussion it seemed to be the general opinion that the incorporation of the Society at present was not desirable, and the motion was thereupon lost. The Court thereupon adjourned.

A meeting of the Council was then held, and business pertaining to the Society was thereupon transacted. The following members constituting the Committee on Membership were then appointed: Bradner Wells Lee, John Randolph Haynes, M. D., George Jules Denis, Frank Putnam Flint, and Harry Woodville Latham. Council then adjourned.

The following delightful menu was then enjoyed by the members of the Society, and the responses to the toasts which followed were listened to with great interest:

Menu....

Clams on Half Shell

Olives　　　　　　Tomatoes　　　　　　Radis

　　　　　　　　Riesling
　　　Potage　　　　Consomme a la Royale

POISSON
Ventre de Saumon, sauce Crevette

Medoc
ENTREES
Ris de veau, sauce Champignons
Cotelettes d'agneau, aux petits pois
Filet de Boeuf larde a la Perigord
Pigeons Braises aux Olives

LEGUMES
Petits Pois　　　　　　Asperges

ROTIS
Cochon de lait, apple sauce

DESSERT
Omelette Soufflee　　Strawberries　　Fruits de la Saison

FROMAGE
Roquefort　　　　Creme　　　　Gruyere
Cafe Royal

Our Country
HOLDRIDGE OZRO COLLINS
Governor of the Society of Colonial Wars in the State of California

King Philip's War
JOHN RANDOLPH HAYNES, M. D.
Surgeon of the Society

Argent, Two Bars Gules
FRANK CLARKE PRESCOTT

The Military Power of the United States
MAJOR WILLIAM ANTHONY ELDERKIN, U. S. A.
Lieutenant Governor of the Society

Auld Lang Syne

The Governor of the Society read the following letter of regret which had been received from the Society of Colonial Dames in the State of California:

To y^e
Honored Governor, and ye Gentlemen o ye First General Courte o ye Commonwealth o Californie.

> Written in ye goodlie
> Cittie o San Francisco
> March ye seventhe
> A. D. 1896.

To y^e
Governor

and companie of ye Firste General Courte o ye Societie o Colonial Wars in ye Commonwealthe o California, Greeting:

Y^e Companie o Coloniale Dames residente in ye State o California through their honored Chairmanne Mistress Selden S. Wright do presente their compliments to ye Gentlemen o ye Firste General Courte. They truste that ye Gentlemen will enacte such Laws as maie be juste and mercifulle and for ye goode of oure faire countrie, and they expresse ye hope that they maie sometime meete ye honored Gentlemen around a hospitable boarde, and discusse a bille o fayre as delectable as that enjoyed by ye Gentlemen o ye Firste General Courte on ye^e eveninge o ye seventhe o Marche in y^e yeare o oure Lorde one thousande eighteen hundrede and ninety-sixe post meridian atte y^e saide Taverne in y^e goodlie cittie o Los Angeles.

With greate respecte, y^e Coloniale Dames o America residente in y^e State o California.

Holdridge Ozro Collins, Governor of the Society, then read the following paper:

OUR COUNTRY.

GENTLEMEN:

It has been said, very wittily, that when our ancestors landed upon this continent they first fell upon their knees, and then upon the aborigines. While this picturesque statement may not be historically correct, at least it strikingly illustrates the characteristics of those ancient worthies, for, with the bible in one hand, and the sword in the other, like Cromwell's Ironsides, they were equally ready to fight or to pray.

In 1620, November 11, old style, the Mayflower anchored at Cape Cod, in what is now Provincetown harbor, and on that date the famous compact was signed, and Bancroft asserts that "this was the birthplace of popular constitutional liberty" (U. S., Vol. I, p. 310). Mr. Goodwin, in his "Pilgrim Republic", says that Provincetown "may justly claim to be the birthplace of the free and equal government which now spans the continent" (p. 65).

"Voltaire said of William Penn's treaty, 'It was the only one ever concluded between savages and christians that was not ratified with an oath, and the only one that was never broken.'

"This is an error. The treaty made at Plymouth in April, 1621, between the Pilgrims and Massasoit, Grand Sachem of the Confederated Tribes of Pokanoket, was ratified by no oath, nor was it broken during the lifetime of any of the contracting parties."

Massosoit died in 1660, leaving two sons, Mooanum, or Wamsutta, and Pomartarken, or Metacom. The General Court at Plymouth gave to Wamsutta the name of Alexander Pokanoket, and to Metacon the name of Philip.

This latter was the Grand Sachem, that heroic Indian Warrior, "King" Philip, whose valorous deeds have a peculiar interest to this Society by reason of the participation of the ancestors of so many of our members in that famous war, which culminated in King Philip's overthrow at the Great Swamp Fight.

The Reverends Merwin and Brewer, Dr. Haynes, Prof. Holden, Mr. Latham and your Governer, have placed upon the records of this Society the story of the participation of their ancestors, soldiers from Massachusetts and Connecticut, in that memorable battle, which secured a permanent relief for those colonies from Indian aggressions.

The story of the development of the dissociated colonies, and their rapid growth into a one harmonious people forms the very acme of romance in our history.

The rugged Puritan, with his stubborn resistance to despotism, insisting upon that liberty for religious observance which he knew to be one of the inalienable rights of his existence; the sturdy Dutchman of New York, who brought from the dykes of his native Holland those institutions of free government which he had saved from the devastating hand of Spanish Phillip, and which to this day form some of the most prominent features of our civil polity; the patient plodding Swede of New Jersey with the memory of his two great Saints—Martin Luther and Gustavus Adolphus—enshrined in his heart; the religious tolerance of the Roman Catholic of Maryland, who, like the Puritan of Connecticut sought a new land for worship in a faith which to him had become broader than a mere ritual; the Scotchman with his rigid adherence to the Covenant, the musical Welshman, the irrepressible Irishman, and the industrious Englishman, all of Pennsylvania; the Cavalier of Virginia, that home of unswerving loyalty to all her ideals, and the mother of that great man who stands as the exemplar for all true Americanism, our own Washington, and the Huguenot of the Carolinas, with his curious combination of Calvanistic predestination and fore-ordination, and the charming ease and gaiety of the mercurial Frenchman, have all become inseparably welded into one great nation, whose people, inheriting those traits of unrelenting fidelity to principle which dominated the actions of their ancestors, and, cherishing their memory with reverential gratitude for the patient endurance of those toils which gave us this noble heritage, have become elevated to a more gentle life, in an environment of higher intellectual culture and more refined social intercourse, and whose lot, we are proud to believe, is the happiest upon the earth.

We are here tonight by reason of the deeds of our ancestors while subjects of England, and fighting under the British flag. For the services of England, in the advancement of political, social and religious liberty throughout the world, no member of this Society, or of the intelligent population of this country will withhold his meed of praise. She has been the great mother of the world to sustain her children in the darkest hours of the advance towards freedom and enlightenment. But this should not blind us to the *certainty*, that the belief, generally prevailing in the United States, that it is to England we owe most of our principles of public polity, and the establishment of those institutions and laws which have elevated us to so high a plane of enlightenment and prosperity, has no foundation in the truth. Hear what Douglas Campbell says:

In Colonial New York "were free schools, the system of recording deeds and mortgages, lands held in common by the towns, all under Dutch rule; here the doctrine was first laid down by a legislative assembly that the *people* are the source of political authority; here were first established permanent religious freedom, the right of petition and the freedom of the press. On the other hand, here were no executions of witches or Quakers, and no kidnaping and enslavement of Indians."

Our country "was settled by men of diverse nationalities. It has always been cosmopolitan. Its institutions differ radically from those of England. The modes of thought of its people are not English."

"Instead of the institutions of the United States being derived from England, it is a curious fact that, while we have in the main, English *social* customs and traits of character, we have scarcely a legal or political institution of importance which is of English origin, and but few which have come to us by the way of England."

"Looking at our legal system today it can almost be said that everything in it consistent with natural justice comes from Rome, and that everything incongruous, absurd and unjust, is a survival of English customs and English legislation."

"Whatever America has accomplished, whether for good or evil, has been largely the result of cutting loose from old English traditions, and developing republican ideas."

(The Puritan in Holland, England and America.)

In the foregoing statement one reservation is made. We are English in our social customs, and the dinner here, as with our British cousins, has become the great factor in the brighter part of our life.

Carlyle says that "the future of the world depends upon cooks," and an English poet has embodied the same idea in his more graceful lines:

" We may live without poetry, music and art ;
We may live without conscience, and live without heart ;
We may live without friends, we may live without books,
But civilized man cannot live without cooks.
He may live without books—what is knowledge but grieving ?
He may live without hope—what is hope but deceiving ?
He may live without love—what is passion but pining ?
But where is the man that can live without dining ?"

Someone once said that were the earth to be blown to pieces, there would be found Englishmen to celebrate the event by a dinner upon one of the fragments.

So we, with our English traits of fellowship, bearing in mind what gentle Izaak Walton says that "it is the company and not the charge that makes the feast," assemble at this table to commemorate the organization of a Society, erected upon a foundation of ancestral association, and whose keystone is our reverence for their heroic deeds. And, as the storm-tossed Pilgrims, after their landing at Plymouth, were greeted by the Mohegan Sachem Samoset with the word "welcome," so, as one of the oldest members of the Society of Colonial Wars, and as Governor in this jurisdiction, I bid you welcome to this reunion; welcome to this board, and welcome to membership in an organization embracing the flower of the intellectual vigor of this land, and recruited from the sons of the makers of this Republic.

I give you this toast:

> Behold my wineglass, 'tis filled to the brim
> With soul-stirring nectar, and I drink it to him
> Who feels, as he kisses its contents away
> It was made to gladden, and not to betray.
> For wine is like woman, and like her was given
> To man on earth as a foretaste of heaven.
> Like her eye it sparkles; like her cheek it glows
> When pressed to the lips of the lover who knows
> How to keep and cherish these treasures of earth;
> For him was woman made, for him the wine's birth.
> Then fill up your glasses, fill quite to the brim,
> And drink with me to the health of him,
> Who feels as he kisses its contents away
> It was made to gladden and not to betray.

And with the words of Macbeth:

> "Come, love and health to all!
> Then I'll sit down. Give me some wine; fill full!
> I drink to the general joy of the whole table."

John Randolph Haynes, M. D., was then introduced by the Governor, and read the following paper on "King Philip's War":

"KING PHILIP'S WAR."

Your Excellency and Members:

THE most important event in the early history of the Colonies was King Philip's War—a fight for existence on the part of the whites and for the annihilation of the hated English on the part of the Indians. This war is, doubtless, of especial interest to the gentlemen present whose ancestors were participants therein. Allow me to recall to your recollection some facts in the antecedent history of the peoples engaged in this conflict.

During the latter part of the sixteenth and the beginning of the seventeenth centuries, in "the golden days of good Queen Bess" and of her treacherous successor, "the gentle Jamie," the English people were divided into Romanists, members of the Church of England, and Dissenters.

The assumption of royalty and the Court party that the occupant of the throne stood in the same relation to the English Church as did the Pope to the Church of Rome, caused the formation of a low Church party, the Puritans, who were ridiculed, persecuted, fined and often imprisoned.

Such, however, is the inconsistency of human nature that the Puritans not only opposed separation from the English Church as a deadly sin, but helped their oppressors to bitterly prosecute, convict and hang the Dissenters or Separatists for their opinions.

The Separatists, our Pilgrim forefathers, believed in the Separation of Church from State, and in the Congregational doctrine as taught today. For boldly advocating their views their property was confiscated. They were reviled and imprisoned, and so inhumanly treated while there, that they died by hundreds from disease, exposure and starvation. Like the Russian of today, in his treatment of the Jews, the Established Church exiled them and hunted them down like wild beasts as they were endeavoring to reach a foreign land. Finally a number reached Holland, where they spent twelve hard, laborious years.

Hearing that they might be merged with the people of the country, they decided to form a new England in a new world.

Thereupon, in 1620, about one hundred men, women and children went to England and embarked in the Mayflower under Captain Jones. After many tribulations and delays and hardships they reached Cape Cod far to the north of the Virginia jurisdiction in which they had a warrant. Before landing, a compact of Government (which was the earliest written constitution in history) was drawn up and signed by the forty-one Pilgrims. After several explorations they landed at Plymouth, December 21st, 1620. Their subsequent suffering from exposure, famine and disease is well known.

The Puritans, in turn, becoming tired of the intolerance of the Church, settled first at Salem in 1628, and then at Boston in 1630. This was the Massachusetts Bay Colony.

Some of the members of this Colony desiring greater religious and political freedom, settled in Rhode Island. Others, from the Massachusetts Colony and Plymouth, wishing more territory, emigrated to Connecticut. In 1643 the Colonies founded a Confederacy for protection against the Indians.

The Indian nations, with whom the Colonists came in contact, occupied about thirty miles of the sea-coast, extending from Maine to the Connecticut River.

The Pequots, the strongest and fiercest of these nations (with the exception of the Mohegans, who, under Uncas, had withdrawn from them) were exceedingly hostile to the whites, and were it not for the enmity that existed between the

Pequots and the next powerful nation, the Narragansetts, their neighbors on the south, the whites and smaller tribes would have been annihilated.

The third important nation was the Pokonoket. Massasoit, of the Wampanoag tribe, was Grand Sachem of this nation, and formed an alliance with the Plymouth Colony for protection against the two stronger nations. This treaty lasted over forty years, and until all parties concerned in it were dead, when it was broken by Massasoit's second son, Philip.

That the Indians were hostile to the Colonists is not to be wondered at. A Captain Hunt visited the coast about six years prior to the coming of the Pilgrims, and seized twenty-seven Indians, taking them to England as slaves.

The pestilence which swept the coast to Narragansett Bay, some years before, had greatly reduced the numbers of the tribes. The further lessening of the Chiefs' power and numbers by proselytism made them jealous and revengeful. Massasoit, the Wampanoag, and Uncas, the Mohegan, although the firm friends of the English, never allowed proselyting among their people when they could prevent it. In 1675 Philip's immediate tribe was limited to three hundred men, women and children.

It is alleged by some that Alexander, Massasoit's elder son, was foully dealt with by the Pilgrims, but this is disproved.

Philip believed, from the sympathy he received from the Puritans when visiting Boston, and from the unfriendly tenor of their remarks when speaking of the Pilgrims, that the Massachusetts Bay Colony would not assist Plymouth.

The occasion of the outbreak was the execution, after a fair trial, of the three Indians who had murdered Sassamon, the Indian preacher.

From the fact that Philip was illy prepared for war—his number being small and his arms few—it is probable he merely contemplated harassing the Colonists with possibly a view to being paid to resume peaceful relations.

The Indians had no just grounds for discontent. The Colonists paid for all lands occupied; succored the Indians; and treated their complaints with such justice, that the settlers complained of the partiality shown them. This policy of conciliation, although perfectly right, probably weakened Philip's respect for the authorities at Plymouth, and may have been one of the causes of the war.

As early as the summer of 1662 rumors of the hostile feeling of the Wampanoags reached the Colonists. Nothing definite occurred, however, until the attack on Swansea in June, 1675. Here the people had abandoned watch to attend a Fast-day service, although a house had been plundered the day before. Ten men were killed, and houses rifled and burned.

Aid was received from Boston, and after ten days pursuit was commenced, when Philip was followed into Mount Hope Peninsula. Then it was found he had paddled across into Pocasset Swamp. The pursuit rested for nearly three weeks. Philip in the meantime killing people and burning houses at Dartmouth and at other villages.

Benjamin Church, the settlers' best Indian fighter, although hampered by the authorities, managed after two skirmishes to drive Philip back into Pocasset Swamp. The Colonists exposing themselves to the enemy, made an attack, but lost five men. Using more caution they drove the savages back into the Swamp, and then, light failing, retired to the neck of the Peninsula. After remaining on guard for ten days with the hope of starving the Indians into surrender, they found that the fighting men had escaped on rafts up the Taunton River, leaving the women and children behind.

They were pursued, thirty Indians killed, and much plunder recovered. The care of this plunder, it is said, caused them to drop the pursuit.

Philip escaped into Central Massachusetts, where he took refuge with the Nipmucks, and from this time on he seemed to take no active part in the war.

The Colonists then warned Canonchet, the Sachem of the Narragansett tribes, not to harbor Philip's women and children. This he refused to do. He had not forgotten that some years before, the Pilgrims had delivered his father, Miantonomo, into the hands of his hereditary enemy, Uncas, the Mohegan, who promptly murdered him. Up to the time of the Pocasset Swamp fight Canonchet had been entirely neutral, but now he withdrew to an island in Cedar Swamp, about ten miles south of Wickford, R. I., where he commenced building extensive and strong fortifications, and prepared for the winter.

The united Colonists, alarmed by rumors that the Indians intended to drive them out of the country in the spring, declared war against the Narragansetts in November, 1675.

One thousand men from Massachusetts Colony, Connecticut and Plymouth, under the command of General Josiah Winslow of Plymouth, met at Pettisquamscot in Rhode Island December 18, 1675, at five o'clock in the afternoon.

The garrison house having been destroyed by Indians a few days before, they encamped in the open field. It was bitterly cold. They broke camp before daybreak, and commenced the march towards the Swamp, ten miles away, in the face of a driving snow-storm, which had set in the night before.

About one o'clock, cold and weary, they came to the edge of the Swamp, where they charged upon the Indians on the outskirts who escaped into the fort.

Crossing the ice (which alone made the fort pregnable, and which the Indians apparently had not taken into account), and guided by an Indian they had captured on the march, they reached a narrow, unfinished corner of the fort. Here they were met by a galling fire (two captains being killed) and repulsed several times.

After the firing had somewhat diminished a grand rush was made for the fort, the entrance taken, and the left flanker captured. The Massachusetts men who were in the lead were now joined by the Connecticut troops in the face of a terrible fire, the right flanker and the block-house were taken. The Indians were driven back, in hand to hand fight, into their camp of wigwams, which proved good intrenchments for them while they fired on the English with deadly effect; and not until the wigwams were fired did the carnage cease. The Plymouth Company and the Massachusetts troops, who had been held in reserve outside in the Swamp, had several skirmishes, but the battle was within the fort.

After the wigwams, with their enormous quantities of provisions had been fired and the Swamp beaten by the troopers for Indians, the little army with its wounded started on its midnight march back to Wickford. It is claimed that some thirty-four wounded men were frozen to death on the homeward march, and that this same march was one of the greatest blunders of the war.

The English lost about sixty-eight men and one hundred and fifty were wounded. Three hundred Indians were killed, and three hundred and fifty men and three hundred women and children taken prisoners in this the crucial battle of the war.

In the spring the war began again. On March 22d, the men at Clark's garrison-house went to church at Plymouth three miles away, leaving the heavy gates open. On their way back they saw their fort burning and found their women and children killed.

Two weeks later, Captain Peirce's fine company of men was destroyed, and in May part of Plymouth was burned.

Philip, turned out by the Nipmucks, returned to Mount Hope where he was surprised by Captain Church and killed.

The death of Philip practically ended the war, though skirmishings were frequent for five months more.

The war was very disastrous to the Colonists. Thirteen towns were destroyed, six hundred houses burned, and six hundred people—mostly able-bodied men—killed. £150,000 worth of property was destroyed, including eight hundred cattle.

From first to last our forefathers' conduct of the war was a series of most stupendous blunders.

Imagine, in an Indian country, during a bloody war, ninety-five fellows escorting some carts of grain, piling their guns upon the carts and scattering through the woods in search of wild grapes. Of course they were killed to a man.

On another occasion, twelve men started for the mill at Springfield, and because their arms were rather heavy to carry, they left them at home. The twelve were killed.

After the great fight the Colonists should have remained in the Indian fort, cared for their wounded, and returned to their homes on a more favorable occasion.

But if ever people were energetic, hardy, long-enduring and lion-hearted, they were; and if we did not regard the memory of our New England ancestors with respect, admiration and loving kindness, we were base ingrates.

For the history in detail of this war I would like to refer you to Goodwin's "Pilgrim Republic", and to the addresses of the Rev. George M. Bodge of Massachusetts, and of Capt. Philip Reed of Illinois, found in the publications of their respective Societies, and which are very interesting reading.

Frank Clarke Prescott then responded to the toast, "Argent, Two Bars Gules", and read the following paper:

ARGENT, TWO BARS GULES.

AS A PATRIOTIC, hereditary society, organized to preserve the memories and landmarks of honored ancestors and their distinguished services, I take it that family heirlooms are not beneath the consideration of the members of the California Society of Colonial Wars. At this First General Court I desire to go on record as endorsing the preservation of the science of heraldry, as being the most graceful and distinctive of the conspicuous features in the life and customs of our forefathers and one of the most valuable pledges we have of the integrity of genealogy.

The precedents for its use in this republic began with the first crusade, continued through the many efforts made to vindicate Christendom in the Holy Land and came down to our own Colonial times unimpaired in its sentimental significance and practical uses adapted to the changing customs of a people evoluting both in methods of dress, government and warfare.

All through the seventeenth and eighteenth centuries the men of dignity and potence in the American colonies, who were laying the broad and deep foundations of liberty and nursing and shaping those characters and sentiments which culminated in the full realization of independence and national pride, were not ashamed to recognize the graceful blazonry which decorated their seals and honored their progenitors.

At the supreme moment when, in obedience to a higher feudal lord, the great American turned against his sovereign, and, true to liberty, severed the old relations, the integrity of family and its evidences were not disturbed, and we find Washington abiding by and continuing the use of *argent, two bars gules*, of his house.

The States, dissenting from tyranny, but loyal to the refinements and memories of their peoples, adopted coats of arms as emblems of sovereignty, and their community possessions or achievements, and the new States to this day preserve the custom.

The federal government, christened in the spirit of prophecy, with the elastic name "United States of America", displayed upon its escutcheon pinions that might wing from Hawaii to Cuba, and teach republican heraldry to more feudal heralds.

And, as though the institution belonged of right in human life and by divine authority, the prophet tells us the Lord spake unto Moses and unto Aaron saying, "Every man of the children of Israel shall pitch by his own standard, with the ensign of their father's house."

Practical use demonstrates the recognition of such signs when every court of record, every corporation, and most public officers whose acts form any historical links in business, land titles or heirship, are required to use seals carefully emblazoned. Searchers of pedigree and those charged with the solving of questions of property rights by succession, concede the value of family coats of arms and artists, dignifying and refining daily lives with tasteful environment, find the crest not too ostentatious for proper effects.

But were the *lion gardent* or the *stag passant* of no greater significance than in the humble function of decorating family plate, there would be no occasion for the criticism of the socialist or the argument of the conservative. The merit in the inherited shield and crest is their indication of pride of ancestry and pledge of fealty to inherited rights. Heraldry, as an emblazoned escutcheon, is a work of art; as an inherited family and national heirloom, it is a sacred sentiment. The *eagle displayed* is a convenient mark on a twenty-dollar gold-piece in the channels of commerce. The same *eagle displayed* may be a pledge of protection to Venezuelan integrity and

Cuban freedom. The charges handed down to us by ancestors who chose them and signalized them in chivalrous valor are pledges of our own fealty to right and justice, to individualize us and put us under such obligations to right government and honorable private life that pride alone will keep us faithful. It is the prescriptive, the permanent, the abiding side of our natures that heraldry in this age appeals to.

Between the socialist and the monarchist, between him who asks a community of goods and lands, and him who sees the golden age in the time of feudal lords and helpless vassals, where is the happy mean? Surely, in a combination of the grace and dignity of the old life and the enlarged freedom and activity of the new.

In the attitude of that statesman who made liberty the synonym of America, and in whom, as he was the highest type of patriot, we should find the pattern for citizenship, and whose character and life should furnish inspiration for modern statecraft, and by whose opinions lines of principle should be drawn, along which the national spirit should develop. The style of man that Washington was, is the style of citizen who will best perpetuate his country's greatness. Not only in Washington the captain, but in Washington the gentleman. Not only in the Washington whose rebellious sword resisted the senseless and criminal obstinacy of his king, but in the Washington who preserved in the simplicities of a republican court the refinements, the graceful honors, the chivalrous valor of the old *regime*. Not only in the Washington who vehemently and abruptly deprecated the suggestion of a crown, but in the Washington whose signet remained to his death "*argent, two bars gules*"; the type of gentleman, of noble, if you please, whose delicacy of patriotism has left the country he founded in doubt as to whether the stars and stripes of its escutcheon were suggested by the bars and mullets of the shield of his family. In this there is the happy medium which would suggest that the graces of the old political life be preserved in the simplicities of the new. Not to temper but to adorn liberty, not to curb but by prescriptive hold on its older forms, to anchor it.

Is it not time, now that the nation has workmen to spare from pioneering, to cease ridiculing those who would polish the corners of the temple? That boorishness cease to be a boast. Washington, in every instinct, sympathized with those men of affairs of the old school whose memories we honor today. He made their spirit of dignified regard for precedent and property rights his inspiration. He endorsed that spirit. We inherit it, and no demagoguery shall intimidate us, if we are true patriots and true gentlemen of this Society, into dangerous concessions to popular clamors of the hour.

Someone has said that politics makes cowards of us all. It is the serious business of this Society, or I misjudge it, to deny the paraphrase and prove that there are those of tried blood who understand the primal personal rights that must be preserved through all the changes of community relations and whose honor is pledged by the ensigns of their father's house.

Heredity is a fact, heraldry, its talismans, need not be ignored.

The part heraldry should play in America is the part Washington gave it—preserved and emphasized to preserve and emphasize the duties chivalrous freedom imposes.

I would not compromise this company by anything heterodox but, conceding the constitutional right of every person to life, liberty and the pursuit of happiness and to equal protection therein according to law, I believe that nature's orders of nobility cannot be abolished, and until the millennium—until the last boor has been made gentle—there must be distinctions of birth, breeding and parts which the vizored helmet will not broaden. I thank heaven that I shall not live to see the day when the social landscape will be a dead level; when the lights and shadows of genius and affection will all be toned down to one dead gray and personal effort, and individual enterprise will be deadened into a treadmill of absolute, uninteresting and unchangeable equality. No coats of arms, no glittering banners, no flashing steel, no lofty mountains, no green valleys, no roaring cataracts or rippling streams, no sunshine, no clouds, no deeds of valor nor sacrifices of affection, no ancestors, no posterity. The millennium of socialism.

Rather give me the pleasing gradations of this evening where I stand amid excellencies that do not rival. Where the ermine, charged with the scales, gives an honored precedence to our Deputy Governor, the Honorable Erskine Mayo Ross. Where comely vigor and manly grace make our Secretary, Harry Woodville Latham, our Appollo Belvidere; and by deeds of valor at the festal board, undismayed among glittering ranks of gory wine glasses, our Chancellor, George Jules Denis, also comely, also vigorous, sits an Appolinaris Belvidere; where His Excellency, Holdridge Ozro Collins, our Governor, accepts and wears gracefully the honors thrust upon him, rather than be thrust out of a fifth-story window. Where I myself, distinguished by a marked individuality most embarrassingly conspicuous as being the only member of the Society who does not have an office, may look forward to the time when my lord, Justice McKinstry, shall come up with me into honorable publicity as a high private and we may sit in banc.

I am not disconcerted, therefore, that in the Society of the Colonial Wars the tapestry is drawn aside and the light falls from out history through stained glass windows charged with the leopard's face and the boar's head, with the chevron and the ermine; that it gleams on a helmet and throws into relief a crest. The stars and stripes have lost no *prestige* in the possibility that the charges of Washington's arms suggested their characteristics. But to the contrary, there seems an added sanctity to that standard which has upon it, in bars and mullets, the pledges of the good faith of the blood of Washington.

Major William Anthony Elderkin, U. S. A., then read the following paper, upon

"THE MILITARY POWER OF THE UNITED STATES."

TO be called upon to respond for "The Army" is an honor and responsibility that I always appreciate, but to-night I feel that the honor and responsibility are intensified, addressing, as I am, descendants of those heroes who, in the Colonial War of 1758, stood their ground, firing from behind trees and stumps, while the regulars of the British army ran past them; and who, without doubt, were the nucleus for the formation of our army, which began its glorious history on the 19th of April, 1775, and which today but awaits the opportunity to add further victories to its already brilliant record.

Our army, when compared with those of the principal foreign nations, is not large in numerical strength. But we must remember that no great nation has so simple a military problem as America. A republican form of government is not compatible with a large and powerful standing army. France, surrounded on every side by enemies, is compelled to maintain one for self-existence. Monarchy, on the other hand, and a large and standing army, are correlative matters. Whereas we have no jealous and threatening neighbors, no inherited race quarrels which are such potent factors in hastening war. We are, by reason of our great numbers and vast territory, absolutely free from all danger of a war of conquest. Our only need, therefore, is that we should be in a condition to discuss international questions with foreign powers without having our greatest cities, and their vast wealth and commercial interests, absolutely at the mercy of those powers.

Gentlemen, when you look back on what our army has done in the past, I do not think you need fear for the future. If, during the Revolution, but 309,781 men were engaged; during the war of 1812, 556,622; during the Mexican War, 112,230, and during the War of the Rebellion, 2,778,304, what is there we could not overcome when you consider the following figures?

The aggregate number of the Regular Army is.............................	28,216
The aggregate number of the Militia is..	116,899
Making a total effective force of...	145,115
To this add the number of men available for military duty (but unorganized), viz:..	9,582,806
Shows a total strength of..	9,727,921

men, or more than three times as many as were engaged during the four years of the Civil War.

Our little standing guard of 28,216 men is the nucleus of a larger and majestic force, which, when the opportunity and necessity arrive, has its own and peculiar duties to perform. The Adjutant-General's department, Quartermaster-General's, Commissary-General's, Surgeon-General's, Inspector-General's, the Corps of Engineers, the Ordinance department, the Signal Corps, and other staff departments, are all well trained in their duties. The Light and Heavy Artillery, the Cavalry, and the Infantry, are all drilled with the utmost care from "Reveille" to "Taps" from daylight to dark. The Military Academy teaches the young military idea how to shoot like officers, and the Military Recruiting Depots to make it shoot like soldiers.

Now, what is it for? What is the expense of $23,279,-402.73, or $800 to $900 per man, for? A regular standing army? No! A nucleus for a larger and majestic force? Yes! that's it. Here 14,000 Infantry, 4,300 Artillery, and 6,604 Cavalry—say 25,000 well drilled men. In two months we can have an army of 2,000,000. Yes! And in four months more than 4,000,000; this being less than half the total number of men available for military duty, but unorganized.

This regular army of ours is the yeast, the leaven which, placed with care, will leaven the whole mass. Each private will make a non-commissioned officer, each non-commissioned officer will make a lieutenant or captain, each captain will make a field-officer, and as for privates we will take them from the sturdy and strong men who know little of war, but are there, "rough and ready" to march and fight, and, if necessary, to fall in defense of the nation's colors — "The Red, White and Blue" — the "Old Glory" — the "Star Spangled Banner" — just as our ancestors did 120 years ago.

A recent estimate of the present position of European powers in the matter of armaments is as follows: At the head of all stands Russia, with an army of 858,000 men in peace times, or a percentage of 9 soldiers to every 1,000 inhabitants. Germany comes next with an effective strength of 580,000 men, which works out at 13 per 1,000. France follows Germany with an army of 512,000 men, or 14 per 1,000. Italy comes next with an effective of 300,000, or 10 per 1,000 inhabitants. While the British army is said to have a total effective of 230,000, and a percentage of 6 per 1000. The Spanish army has 100,000 effectives, or a percentage of 6 soldiers per 1,000 inhabitants. These figures are interesting for comparison.

I will ask you to excuse me, gentlemen, for now taking you back to the year 218 B. C. — it is a long time ago — but I want to draw your attention to what was done by an army smaller than our own. I refer to the Carthagenian army, when, with Hannibal in command, it at last stood safely in the valley of the Po ready to start on its great errand of avenging the disgrace and misfortune inflicted on its country in the great Punic War. How Hannibal, with only 26,000 men, braved the Roman armies even when they outnumbered his, more than *four* to *one*, and with his often half-starved and ill-supplied forces breathed defiance against Rome for half a generation.

My object in referring to this page of ancient history is that I may allay the anxiety of any of you, dear friends, who within the past few minutes have been performing mental calculations with the figures I have just given you, and discovered that some of the nations I mentioned outnumbered our forces to the extent that the Romans outnumbered Hannibal's. The moral I want to draw is this: If the antiquated Captain was able, in the year 218 B. C., to hold his own against such odds, you certainly need have no fear but that Major-General N. A. Miles, with his command of 28,216 men, can "*go him one better*" in the year 1896, A. D.

George Jules Denis was then introduced by the Governor and delivered a bright and witty extemporaneous speech, in which he generally and in a happy style, discussed the various papers which had been read. The exercises were then brought to a close by the singing of "Auld Lang Syne".

In Memoriam.

✠

HARRY WOODVILLE LATHAM, the first Secretary and a charter member of this Society, was born in Lynchburg, Virginia, on September 30, 1862, and died at his home in Pasadena, Los Angeles County, California, on May 14, 1896. He was the son of Mr. George W. Latham who, during the Civil War, served upon the staff of General Robert E. Lee. His maternal grandfather was Mr. Philo Calhoun, for many years president of the First National Bank of New York, a man widely known and respected.

Mr. Latham's boyhood was spent at Bridgeport, Connecticut, where his family then resided. He entered Yale College in 1879, graduating with honors in the class of 1883. While at Yale he was a member of the principal college societies, and took a prominent part in athletics. After his graduation at Yale, he took the regular course of study at the Columbia College Law School, New York, and graduated therefrom. Upon his graduation, he was admitted to the bar and entered the law office of Seward, Griswold, Guthrie & Da Costa, New York, where he spent some time in the practice of his profession.

Owing to ill health in 1887, he came to California, and in 1889 he established himself in the practice of the law at Los Angeles. In 1891 he formed a partnership with M. L. Graff, Esq., and the firm thereupon became attorneys for the Board of Trade.

Mr. Latham was a faithful and consistent member of St. Paul's Protestant Episcopal Church, Los Angeles, of which organization he had been for several years a valued vestryman and trustee. He was also secretary and a member of the Board of Trustees of the Hospital of the Good Samaritan. He was also a member of the Society of the Sons of the Revolution in California, and also a member of the Sunset Club, and of the California Club, and took a prominent part in social life. He was a deservedly popular young man, a faithful and wise counselor, a hard student, and one who was rapidly attaining distinction in his chosen profession.

The bar of Los Angeles, at a special meeting, adopted resolutions of respect, which were spread upon the minutes of the Superior Court, and also of the United States Circuit Court and the United States District Court, at Los Angeles. A committee of the bar was appointed to attend his funeral, with a like committee from the Society of the Sons of the Revolution, and a like committee from this Society.

The Board of Trade of Los Angeles also adopted resolutions expressing their high regard for the character of Mr. Latham, and their deep sense of loss at his early demise.

The funeral occurred on May 22, 1896, from his home in Pasadena, and the remains were subsequently sent to Bridgeport, Conn., for interment.

Mr. Latham was the first secretary of this Society, and took an active part and deep interest in its organization and in the objects for which the Society was organized.

He exemplified in a marked degree those sterling qualities and devotion to duty which characterized the sturdy Puritans of New England from some of whose distinguished citizens he was a lineal and worthy descendant. He was withal a man of integrity and that sweetness of temper, and gentlemanly bearing which attracted and endeared him to his friends.

MEMBERSHIP.

7. BREWER, REV. WILLIAM AUGUSTUS.

Seventh in descent from Lieut. Thomas Tracy, 1610–1685. Ensign First Train Band, Norwich, Conn., 1666; and in 1672, Lieutenant in the New London County Dragoons, enlisted to fight the Dutch and Indians. Member of the General Court of Connecticut twenty-seven sessions. Commissary in King Philip's War.

Seventh in descent from Lieut. Thomas Leffingwell, 1622–1657. Rendered important aid to "Uncas", when the latter was besieged by hostile Indians. Lieutenant of the Norwich, Conn., Train Band, 1672; served in King Philip's War; also served in Capt. Denison's famous band of Indian fighters. Deputy to the General Court, 1661–1710, Colony of Connecticut.

1. COLLINS, HOLDRIDGE OZRO.

Ninth in descent from Stephen Hart, 1605–1683. Served in Capt. John Mason's Command through the Pequot War of 1637. Deputy from Farmington to the General Court, 1647, 1655, 1660, Colony of Conn.

Ninth in descent from John Plumb, 1594–1648. Served in Capt. Mason's Command in the Pequot War, 1637. Deputy from Wethersfield to the General Court from 1636 to 1642, Colony of Conn.

Ninth in descent from Hugh Calkin, 1600–1690. Deputy from Gloucester to the General Court, 1650–1651, Colony of Massachusetts Bay. Deputy to the General Court from New London and Norwich twenty-two sessions, from 1652 to 1690, Colony of Conn.

Eighth in descent from William Hough,—1683. He was
sergeant in the first Military Company of New London.
Appointed by the General Court of Connecticut, October,
1675, engineer to erect fortifications in New London
during King Philip's War.

Eighth in descent from John Bronson, —1680. Soldier in
command of Capt. John Mason during the Pequot War,
and participated in the great battle of May 26, 1637. Deputy to the General Court from Farmington, 1651, and
subsequently. Colony of Conn.

Eighth in descent from Mathese Blanchan. Served in command of Capt. Martin Kregier in the rescuing expedition
against the Indians after the massacre at Esopus, New
York, June 7, 1663.

Seventh in descent from Cornelis Barentsen Slecht, —1671.
One of the nine signers of the agreement dated May 31,
1658, with Governor Peter Stuyvesant for the settlement
of Wiltwyck, and Sergeant of the first Military company
of that place. Appointed on May 16, 1661, one of the
first three "Schepens" of Esopus, the other two being
Evert Pels and Albert Heymans Roosa, and who, with
the "Schout" Roeloff Swartwout, composed the first
Court of Justice in Ulster County, New York. He
fought at the Indian Massacre at Wiltwyck on June 7,
1663, when his children were taken captive, and he served
under Captain Martin Kregier in the rescuing expedition
which effected their recovery. "He, from the beginning,
took a prominent and active part in the affairs of the
Church and settlement."

Seventh in descent from Louis Du Bois, 1627-1696. Served in
command of Capt. Martin Kregier in the rescuing expedition against the Indians after the massacre at Esopus,
New York, June 7, 1663.

Seventh in descent from David Provoost, 1608-1656. Commander of Fort Good Hope, 1642-1647; one of the

"Nine Men" in 1652; Sergeant of the "Blue Flag Company" of the Burgher Corps of New Amsterdam, 1652, Colony of New Netherland.

Seventh in descent from Anthony Thompson, —1647. Signer of the "Compact" with Gov. Eaton and the Rev. John Davenport at New Haven, June 4th, 1639. Soldier in the Indian troubles, 1642, 1643, 1644, Colony of New Haven.

Seventh in descent from Arthur Perry, —1652. Member of the Ancient and Honorable Artillery Company of Boston.

Seventh in descent from John Lewis, Jr., 1655–1717. Sergeant of the New London, Conn., Train Band; killed 1717.

Seventh in descent from Samuel Hickox, Sr.,—1695. Sergeant of the Waterbury, Conn., Train Band, 1686–1695. Died at his post in the discharge of his military duties.

Seventh in descent from Isaac Bronson, 1645–1719. Sergeant of the Waterbury Train Band, 1695. Deputy from Waterbury to the General Court, 1697–1701, Colony of Conn.

Seventh in descent from Stephen Upson, Sr., 1653–1735. Deputy to the General Court from Waterbury, 1710, 1712, 1729, Colony of Conn. Sergeant of the Waterbury, Conn., Train Band, 1715.

Sixth in descent from Stephen Upson, Jr., 1686–1777. Deputy to the General Court from Waterbury, 1743, 1763, 1765, 1766, and Captain of Militia, Colony of Conn.

Sixth in descent from Abraham DuBois, 1657–1731. Served in the Second Military Expedition against the French in Canada, 1717.

Sixth in descent from Roeloff Swartwout, 1634–1715. "Schout" of Esopus during Indian War of 1663, and member of the Council of Gov. Jacob Leisler, 1689, Colony of New Netherland and New York.

Sixth in descent from Capt. Arie Roosa, 1650—. Captain of a foot company in the Ulster and Dutchess Counties Regiment, commanded by Lieut.-Col. Jacob Rutsen, 1700.

Fifth in descent from Lieut. Jonathan Beebe, 1709-1760. First Lieutenant, Seventh Company, Second Connecticut Regiment, 1759. Served with distinction in the French and Indian War, at Crown Point, Lake George and Ticonderoga.

24. COLTON, ALLEN LYSANDER.

Eighth in descent from George Colton. Quartermaster of the Massachusetts Militia, 1669, 1671 and 1677. Deputy to the General Court, Colony of Massachusetts Bay.

2. DENIS, GEORGE JULES.

Sixth in descent from William Hall, —1714. Representative to the Assembly of West Jersey, 1697 and 1701. Appointed Justice of the Court of Common Pleas, 1699. Royal Councillor of the Province of New Jersey, 1708-1713.

3. ELDERKIN, WILLIAM ANTHONY, Lieut.-Col. U. S. A.

Fourth in descent from Col. Jedediah Elderkin, 1717-1793. Deputy from Windham to the General Court, 1751-1785, Colony of Conn. Col. Fifth Regiment Connecticut Militia, March, 1775.

4. FENNER, CHARLES PUTNAM.

Eighth in descent from Thomas Buckingham, —1657. Deputy to the General Court, 1657, New Haven Colony.

Fourth in descent from Rufus Putnam, 1738-1824. Private, 1757, in Col. Fry's Massachusetts Regiment. Private, 1758, in Col. Ruggles' Massachusetts Regiment. Sergeant, 1759, in Col. Ruggles' Massachusetts Regiment. Ensign, 1760, in Col. Willard's Massachusetts Regiment, French and Indian War. Served at Saratoga, Fort Edward, Ticonderoga, and Lake Champlain. Brigadier-General, Continental Army.

22. FLINT, FRANK PUTNAM.

Sixth in descent from Thomas Flint, 1645-1721. Soldier in King Philip's War. In Capt. Gardner's Company in service against Narragansetts in 1675.

21. FLINT, MOTLEY HEWES.

Sixth in descent from Thomas Flint, 1645-1721. Soldier in King Philip's War. In Captain Gardner's Company in service against Narragansetts in 1675.

8. HARDEN, EDWARD THOMAS.

Fifth in descent from Col. John Palmer, —1740. Colonel in command of expedition from South Carolina against Yemasse Indians, in Florida, 1727. Aide-de-camp to Gov. Oglethorpe, in campaign against St. Augustine, and killed at Fort Moosa, June 14, 1740.

Fourth in descent from Benjamin Baker, 1717-1785. Soldier from Georgia in the army of Gov. Oglethorpe, in campaign against St. Augustine, Fla., 1740.

19. HAYNES, JOHN RANDOLPH.

Sixth in descent from Ephraim Fellows, 1639—. Trooper in company of Capt. Nicholas Page from Massachusetts, and participated in the "Great Swamp Fight", December 19, 1675.

16. HOLDEN, EDWARD SINGLETON.

Seventh in descent from Maj.-Gen. Humphrey Atherton,-1661. Deputy from Dorchester to the General Court of Massachusetts, 1638, and nine times afterwards. Speaker, 1653. Assistant, 1654-1661. Lieutenant, 1645. Captain, 1646. Commander of the Ancient and Honorable Artillery Company, 1650. Commanded expedition against Pesoacus, a Narragansett Chief, 1650. Major-General, 1661.

Seventh in descent from William Blake, 1594–1663, of Dorchester, Mass. A member of the Ancient and Honorable Artillery Company of Boston.

Sixth in descent from Justinian Holden, 1613–1691. A soldier from Massachusetts in King Philip's War, 1676.

9. Latham, Harry Woodville, Deceased May 14, 1896.

Eighth in descent from Capt. Thomas Fitch, 1630–1690. Ensign, 1665. Commissioner, 1669. Captain, 1673, and in King Philip's War. Deputy-Governor, 1673, Colony of Conn.

Eighth in descent from Matthew Mitchell, 1590–1645. Deputy to the General Court, May, 1637, which voted "that there should be an offensive warr against the Pequoitt". Trumbull says that "The measures taken by the Court were so spirited that the names of its members deserve perpetuation". Assistant, 1638. Served in the garrison at Saybrook Fort, under Lion Gardner, in the Pequot War. Served in an encounter with the Indians on the Connecticut River, when his brother-in-law, Samuel Butterfield, was killed, October, 1636. Mather says, "His buildings were twice burned by Indians, his cattle destroyed, and his estate to the value of some hundreds of pounds damnified, so that his family suffered more from the Pequot scourge than any in the land".

Eighth in descent from Thomas Sherwood, 1586–1655. Deputy to the General Court of Connecticut, 1645.

Seventh in descent from Joseph Hawley, 1603–1690. Deputy to the General Court of Connecticut eleven terms, between 1665 and 1687.

Seventh in descent from Samuel Sherman, 1618–1684. Deputy to the General Court, May, 1637, which declared that "There should be an offensive warr against the Pequoitt". Trumbull says that "The measures taken by this Court were so spirited that the names of its members deserve perpetuation". Assistant, 1663–1668. Appointed by the General Court, July 6, 1665, one of a committee to defend the coast from Stratford to Rye, against the Dutch, under Admiral De Reuter, Colony of Conn.

Sixth in descent from Capt. David Sherman, 1665-1753. Ensign of Stratfield, Conn., Train Band, 1703. Lieutenant, 1708. Captain, 1709. Deputy to the General Court, Conn., from Fairfield, 1709.

10. LEE, BRADNER WELLS.

Ninth in descent from Ensign Hugh Welles, 1590-1645. Born in Essex County, England; died in Wethersfield, Conn. Ensign of the Wethersfield, Conn., Train Band.

Seventh in descent from Ensign Noah Welles, 1666-1712. Ensign of New London, Conn., Train Band, 1703.

14. MERWIN, REV. ALEXANDER MOSS.

Seventh in descent from Gov. Robert Treat, 1622-1710. Commander at the "Great Swamp Fight". Major commanding Connecticut troops at the battles of Hadley and Springfield. Deputy-Governor, 1676-1686. Appointed Governor, 1686, resigned, 1701. In the encounter with the Indians at Bloody Brook, September 18, 1675, his arrival with the Connecticut troops gained the victory.

20. MCKINSTRY, ELISHA WILLIAMS.

Seventh in descent from Governor William Bradford, 1589-1657. Governor of Plymouth Colony.

5. NICHOLS, HENRY ATHERTON.

Tenth in descent from Gov. Thomas Dudley, 1576-1653. Second Governor of Massachusetts Bay Colony, 1634-1640, 1645, 1650. Deputy-Governor, 1630, 1634, 1637-1640, 1646-1650, 1651-1652. Assistant, 1635-1636, 1641-1644. In office continuously twenty-two years. Commissioner for the United Colonies, 1643, 1647, 1649, and twice President of the United Colonies. Major-General, 1646. Signed the charter of Harvard College, 1650.

Ninth in descent from Daniel Denison, 1612–1682. Captain Massachusetts troops in the Pequot War, 1637. Major-General, 1652–1680. Deputy to the General Court, Massachusetts, 1635–1652. Colonial Secretary, 1653. Commissioner for United Colonies, 1654–1662.

Eighth in descent from John Gilman, 1624–1708. Lieutenant of Exeter, New Hampshire, Militia, 1708; member of the First Council of the Province of New Hampshire, 1680; member of Assembly, 1693–1697. Speaker of the House in 1695. Captain of Exeter, New Hampshire, Militia.

6. NICHOLS, WILLARD ATHERTON.

Ninth in descent from Gov. Thomas Dudley, 1576–1653. Second Governor of Massachusetts Bay Colony, 1634–1640, 1645, 1650. Deputy Governor, 1630, 1634, 1637–1640, 1646–1650, 1651–1652. Assistant, 1635–1636, 1641–1644. In office continuously twenty-two years. Commissioner for the United Colonies, 1643, 1647, 1649, and twice President of the United Colonies. Major-General, 1646. Signed the charter of Harvard College, 1650.

Eighth in descent from Daniel Denison, 1612–1682. Captain Massachusetts troops in the Pequot War, 1637; Major-General, 1652–1680; Deputy to the General Court, Mass., 1635–1652. Colonial Secretary, 1653. Commissioner for the United Colonies, 1654–1662.

Seventh in descent from John Gilman, 1624–1708. Lieutenant of Exeter, New Hampshire, Militia, 1708; member of the First Council of the Province of New Hampshire, 1680; member of Assembly, 1693–1697. Speaker of the House in 1695. Captain of Exeter, New Hampshire, Militia.

11. OSGOOD, JOSIAH ALONZO. (Resigned March 7, 1896.)

Sixth in descent from Capt. John Osgood, Jr., 1630-1693. Sergeant, 1658-1661; Lieutenant, 1666-1668; Captain, 1683, Massachusetts Militia; Deputy from Andover, Mass., to the General Court, 1668, 1669, 1689, 1690.

23. PAYSON, ALBERT HENRY.

Seventh in descent from Philip Eliot, 1602-1657. Member of the Ancient and Honorable Artillery Company of Boston, Mass., 1638. Deputy to the General Court Colony of Massachusetts Bay.

15. PRESCOTT, FRANK CLARKE.

Ninth in descent from Gov. Thomas Dudley, 1576-1653. Second Governor of Massachusetts Bay Colony, 1634, 1640, 1645, 1650. Deputy-Governor, 1630, 1634, 1637-1640, 1646-1650, 1651-1652. Assistant, 1635-1636, 1641-1644. In office continuously twenty-two years. Commissioner for the United Colonies, 1643, 1647, 1649, and twice President of the United Colonies. Major-General, 1646. Signed the charter of Harvard College, 1650.

17. ROSS, ERSKINE MAYO.

Fourth in descent from John Mayo, 1737-1792. Member of Virginia House of Burgesses from Chesterfield County in 1769, 1770, 1771, 1775, and from Henrico County in 1772. Member of the Conventions of 1775 and 1776.

18. THOM, CAMERON ERSKINE.

Third in descent from John Mayo, 1737-1792. Member of Virginia House of Burgesses from Chesterfield County in 1769, 1770, 1771, 1775, and from Henrico County in 1772. Member of the Conventions of 1775 and 1776.

12. THORPE, ANDREW ROANE.

Fifth in descent from Patrick Henry, 1736–1799. Member of Virginia House of Burgesses, 1765–1783; member of First Continental Congress, September 4, 1774; first Governor of the State of Virginia.

13. THORPE, SPENCER ROANE.

Fourth in descent from Patrick Henry, 1736–1799. Member of the Virginia House of Burgesses, 1765–1783; member of First Continental Congress, September 4, 1774; first Governor of the State of Virginia.

Society of Colonial Wars,
In the State of California.
INSTITUTED NOVEMBER 30, 1895.

Information for Applicants.

Qualification for Membership.

Any male person above the age of twenty-one years, of good moral character and reputation, shall be eligible to membership in the Society of Colonial Wars in the State of California, who is lineally descended in the male or female line from an ancestor:

(1) Who served as a military or naval officer, or as a soldier, sailor, or marine, or as a privateersman, under authority of the Colonies which afterward formed the United States, or in the forces of Great Britain which participated with those of the said Colonies in any wars in which the said colonies were engaged, or in which they enrolled men, from the settlement of Jamestown, May 13th, 1607, to the battle of Lexington, April 19th, 1775; or

(2) Who held office in any of the Colonies between the dates mentioned, either as

(a) Director-General, Vice-Director-General, or member of the Council or legislative body, in the Colony of New Netherland;

(b) Governor, Lieutenant or Deputy Governor, Lord Proprietor, member of the King's or Governor's Council or legislative body, in the Colonies of New York, New Jersey, Virginia, Pennsylvania and Delaware;

(c) Lord Proprietor, Governor, Deputy Governor, or member of the Council or legislative body, in Maryland and the Carolinas;

(d) Governor, Deputy Governor, Governor's Assistant, or Commissioner to the United Colonies of New England, or member of the Council, body of assistants, or legislative body in any of the New England Colonies.

Requirements.

No application for membership will be accepted based only on traditional statements, nor unless such statement be accompanied by a paged reference to public records or recognized authority, authenticating such service or rank, or when proof depends upon private documents, by copies duly authenticated of such documents.

Applications must be in duplicate, properly filled out and signed by two members of this Society.

It is a rule of the Council, that Candidates residing in the City of Los Angeles and vicinity be personally known to some gentleman of the Council before action will be taken on their names.

A check for initiation fee and first year's dues must accompany the application for membership.

Expense of Membership and Insignia.

Initiation Fee	$ 10.00
Annual Dues	5.00
Life Membership	50.00
Perpetual Membership	250.00
Certificate of Membership from General Society	5.00
Insignia in Gold	26.00
Insignia in silver gilt	16.00
Rosette	.25
Supplemental Application blanks, per set	.25

Application blanks may be obtained from the secretary.

When the applicant derives eligibility of membership by descent from more than one ancestor, and it is desired to take advantage thereof, "Supplemental Application Blanks," should be obtained, *and* in *each* case made out and filed with the original.

No supplemental applications will be considered until the applicant shall have become a member of the Society.

The Insignia and Certificate of Membership are issued by the General Society, and their purchase is optional.

Rosettes may be obtained from the Secretary and Treasurer.

HARRY WOODVILLE LATHAM, *Secretary.*
Los Angeles, Cal.

FRANK PUTNAM FLINT, *Treasurer.*
Los Angeles, Cal.

Officers, Gentlemen of the Council and Committee on Membership.
1896.

Governor,
HOLDRIDGE OZRO COLLINS.

Deputy Governor,
HON. ERSKINE MAYO ROSS.

Lieutenant Governor,
MAJOR WILLIAM ANTHONY ELDERKIN, U. S. A.

Secretary,
HARRY WOODVILLE LATHAM.

Treasurer,
FRANK PUTNAM FLINT.

Registrar,
EDWARD THOMAS HARDEN.

Historian,
BRADNER WELLS LEE.

Chancellor,
GEORGE JULES DENIS.

Surgeon,
JOHN RANDOLPH HAYNES, M. D.

Chaplain,
REV. ALEXANDER MOSS MERWIN.

Gentlemen of the Council,
SPENCER ROANE THORPE, *Chairman.*

REV. WILLIAM AUGUSTUS BREWER. WILLARD ATHERTON NICHOLS.
CHARLES PUTNAM FENNER.
MOTLEY HEWES FLINT. CAMERON ERSKINE THOM.
HENRY ATHERTON NICHOLS.
ANDREW ROANE THORPE. FRANK CLARKE PRESCOTT.

Committee on Membership
GEORGE JULES DENIS.
FRANK PUTNAM FLINT. JOHN RANDOLPH HAYNES, M. D.
HARRY WOODVILLE LATHAM. BRADNER WELLS LEE.

Deputy Governor Genearl.
SPENCER ROANE THORPE.

Eureka.

Society of Colonial Wars,
in the
State of California.

Office of the Registrar.

Dear Sir:

At a Special Court of this Society, the following Resolutions were unanimously adopted, viz.:

"RESOLVED: That all of the members of this Society be and they are hereby requested to deliver to the Registrar their autobiographies embracing the principal events of their lives, and such other occurrences in their experiences as they may desire to have perpetuated, for the use of the Society, or the information of their children, and that said autobiographies be spread at large upon the records of the Registrar.

"RESOLVED: That the same be printed in suitable shape under the direction of the Historian when the amount of money in the Treasury shall warrant such an expense.

"The members are further requested to forward to the Registrar their photographs in cabinet size. Said photographs shall be preserved in suitable albums among the records and archives of the Society."

The plan set forth in the foregoing Resolutions, of having the personal history of the members perpetuated upon our records, has met with the general approval of the gentlemen of this Society.

It is intended that these biographies shall cover only the personal experiences of our members, and not embrace any facts concerning their ancestors, as provision is made, under Article XXI of the By-Laws, for an Ancestral Record.

It is earnestly hoped that you will prepare and forward to the Registrar, without delay, the history of your life containing the most marked events, such as date and place of birth; where educated; what College degrees or other honors have been conferred upon you; your profession or avocation; offices held; maiden name of wife; place and date of marriage; names and dates of birth of children, etc., etc.

The collection of photographs of our members has become very interesting, and we trust you will not delay in forwarding a cabinet size photograph of yourself, with your autograph upon the face of the card.

We require the cabinet size photographs as this is the most convenient dimension for preservation in albums.

Trusting you will give these matters your immediate attention, I have the honor to subscribe myself,

Yours very sincerely,

Registrar of the Society of Colonial Wars
in the State of California.

Society
of
Colonial Wars
in the
State of California.

By-Laws

of the

Society of Colonial Wars

of the

State of California.

1896

Nostra Tuebimur Ipsi

THE Code of By-Laws of the Society of Colonial Wars in the State of California was adopted at its First General Court held in the city of Los Angeles on the seventh day of March, 1896.

The untimely death of the Secretary, Harry Woodville Latham, has filled our hearts with sorrow that so bright a young life should be taken from us in the midst of his usefulness. All of the work of the Society properly falling to the duties of his office, has been necessarily delayed, but there is so general a demand for copies of the By-Laws, that I have thought it best to have them issued at once, and not to postpone their publication to an indefinite future. I therefore certify to the correctness of this printed copy of the By-Laws without waiting for the election of a Secretary, to whom such an attestation more properly belongs.

HOLDRIDGE OZRO COLLINS,
Governor.

Los Angeles, Cal., June 15, 1896.

By-Laws

of the

Society of Colonial Wars

of the

State of California.

Preamble.

THE SOCIETY OF COLONIAL WARS IN THE STATE OF CALIFORNIA has been organized for the purpose of perpetuating the memory of those events and of the men who, in military, naval and civil positions of high trust and responsibility, by their acts and counsel assisted in the establishment, defense and preservation of the American Colonies, and were the founders of this Nation; to collect and preserve manuscripts, rolls, relics and records: to provide suitable commemorations or memorials relating to the American Colonial period, and to inspire in its members the fraternal and patriotic spirit of their forefathers, and in the community, respect and reverence for those whose public services made our freedom and unity possible.

We acknowledge the supremacy of the General Society in all matters which have been and which shall be delegated to it, and we pledge ourselves to observe and maintain all laws, rules and regulations for the government and control of the United State Societies, which shall be lawfully prescribed by the General Society.

Now, for the better government of this Society, and the achievement of the ends desired, we have adopted the following Code of By-Laws:

Article I.
NAME.

THE Society shall be known by the name and title of "Society of Colonial Wars in the State of California."

Article II.
MEMBERSHIP.

ANY male person above the age of twenty-one years, of good moral character and reputation, shall be eligible to membership in the Society of Colonial Wars in the State of California, who is lineally descended in the male or female line from an ancestor:

(1.) Who served as a military or naval officer, or as a soldier, sailor or marine, or a privateersman, under authority of the Colonies which afterward formed the United States, or in the forces of Great Britain which participated with those of the said Colonies in any wars in which the said Colonies were engaged, or in which they enrolled men, from the settlement of Jamestown, May 13th, 1607, to the battle of Lexington, April 19th, 1775; or,

(2.) Who held office in any of the Colonies between the dates mentioned, either as

(a) Director-General, Vice-Director-General, or member of the Council or legislative body in the Colony of New Netherland;

(b) Governor, Lieutenant or Deputy-Governor, Lord Proprietor, member of the King's or Governor's Council or legislative body in the Colonies of New York, New Jersey, Virginia, Pennsylvania and Delaware;

(c) Lord Proprietor, Governor, Deputy-Governor, or member of the Council, or of the legislative body in Maryland and the Carolinas;

(d) Governor, Deputy-Governor, Governor's Assistant, or Commissioner to the United Colonies of New England, or member of the Council, body of assistants, or legislative body in any of the New England Colonies.

Article III.

OFFICERS.

THE officers of this Society shall be a Governor, a Deputy-Governor, a Lieutenant-Governor, a Deputy-Governor General, a Secretary, a Treasurer, a Registrar, a Historian, a Chaplain, a Chancellor and a Surgeon, who shall be *ex officio* members of the Council.

Article IV.

GENTLEMEN OF THE COUNCIL AND COMMITTEES.

THERE shall be a Council, consisting of nine members, who shall be styled "Gentlemen of the Council," in addition to the *ex officio* members; a Committee on Membership, consisting of five members; a Committee on Historical Documents, consisting of three members, and a Committee on Entertainment, consisting of five members.

Article V.

ELECTION OF OFFICERS.

THE officers, together with the Gentlemen of the Council, the delegates and alternates to the General Society, and members of all the Standing Committees, except the Committee on Membership and the Deputy-Governor General, shall be elected by ballot at the General Court. A plurality vote shall elect, and said officers and committees shall hold office for one year, or until their successors shall be duly elected and qualified.

Vacancies among the officers, or in the Council or Committees, shall be filled for the residue of the current year at any meeting of the Council called for that purpose.

Provided: That in case there shall be a vacancy in the

office of Governor, the Deputy-Governor, and in case of his inability to act, the Lieutenant-Governor shall thereupon succeed to said office of Governor.

The Deputy-Governor General shall be elected by the delegates to the General Society.

Article VI.

COUNCIL.

THE Council may provide by resolution for regular meetings, but it may be convened at the call of the Governor or Secretary, or upon the written request of three of its members. Five shall be a quorum for the transaction of business. It shall have general control and management of the affairs and funds of the Society, and it may appoint such special committees as to it may seem proper, composed wholly or in part of members of the Society outside of its own number. The Council, for cause, may suspend any officer, and its action must be reported, in writing, to the Society for approval or the reverse, within thirty days thereafter.

Article VII.

COMMITTEE ON MEMBERSHIP.

THE Committee on Membership shall be chosen by the Gentlemen of the Council, and shall be elected for one year. Three members shall constitute a quorum, and a negative vote of one member shall cause an adverse report to the Council upon the application of any candidate.

The proceedings of the Committee shall be secret and confidential. It shall have power to elect from its members a Chairman and Secretary, and to establish regulations for its government not inconsistent with the by-laws of the Society.

Any member failing to attend three successive meetings without sufficient excuse, shall be dropped from the committee, and the Council shall fill the vacancy caused thereby.

Article VIII.
COMMITTEE ON HISTORICAL DOCUMENTS.

THE Committee on Historical Documents, in connection with the Historian, who shall be *ex-officio* chairman, may prepare papers on matters of interest to the Society, and submit them to the Council. No paper shall be printed without the order of the Council. It shall use all possible efforts to secure original documents, muster-rolls and other papers or articles connected with the Colonial history of the country. It shall be empowered to correspond in the name of the Society with individuals, societies and governments, in the course of its investigations. It shall keep a record of its transactions.

Article IX.
COMMITTEE ON ENTERTAINMENT.

THE Committee on Entertainment shall be the Stewards of the Society's banquets, but must present to the Governor a list of all speakers and invited guests for his approval.

They shall have power to select places for banquets, and to issue tickets for the same, but they shall assume no expense without the approval of the Council.

They shall have charge of the annual election, and shall install the officers elected.

Article X.
ELECTION OF MEMBERS.

EVERY application for membership shall be made in writing, subscribed by the applicant under oath or affirmation, upon blanks prescribed by the Council, and approved by two members of the Society over their signatures Applications shall be accompanied by proofs of eligibility, and shall be referred to the Committee on Membership, who shall carefully investigate the same and report their recommendation thereon to the Council.

Members may be elected at any meeting of the Council, but one negative vote of every five ballots cast shall cause the rejection of the candidate.

A rejected candidate shall not be permitted to apply for membership until the lapse of one year, except by the unanimous consent of the Committee on Membership and the Gentlemen of the Council.

Payment of the membership fee and dues for the current year shall accompany the application. In case the candidate shall be rejected, the amount paid by him shall be returned.

Membership shall be hereditary for all male descendants of the present members of this Society, and of those who may hereafter be elected, up to the limit that the Society may hereafter determine upon, subject to the vote of the Council upon the moral qualification of the person who may be an heir at any time to such membership.

Article XI.

DECLARATION.

EVERY applicant for membership shall declare upon honor that he will use his best efforts to promote the purposes of the Society, and will observe the Constitution and By-Laws of the same; and if a citizen of the United States, he shall declare that he will support the Constitution of the United States. Such declaration shall be in writing, and subscribed by the applicant.

Article XII.

RESIGNATION, DISQUALIFICATION AND EXPULSION.

NO resignation of any member shall become effective unless consented to by the Council.

No person who has become enrolled as a member of this Society shall be permitted to continue in membership after his proofs of eligibility shall have been found to be defective.

After six months' notice to such person to substantiate

his claim, and upon his failure satisfactorily so to do, the Council must direct the Secretary to erase his name from the membership roll.

The said person shall have the right to appeal to the Society at its next Court or to the General Court. If the said appeal be sustained by a two-thirds vote of the members present at such Court, his name shall be restored to said membership roll.

Any member, for conduct inconsistent with the character of a gentleman and man of honor, or for serious disloyalty to this Society, or for other grave cause, may be suspended or expelled from the Society. But no member shall be suspended or expelled unless written charges are presented against him. The Council, after hearing such charges, and giving him an opportunity to reply to them, may act by a two-thirds vote, and its action shall be final. The insignia of said member shall thereupon be returned to the Treasurer of the Society, and his rights therein shall be extinguished or suspended. The Treasurer shall refund to said member the amount paid for said insignia.

Article XIII.
PURPOSES.

AT every meeting of the Council the purposes and general welfare of the Society shall be considered, and measures taken to promote and secure them. No party political question of the day, nor existing controversial religious subject shall be discussed or considered in the Council, or at any meeting of this Society, or of any of its committees.

Article XIV.
COMMEMORATIONS.

THE Society shall celebrate yearly some event in Colonial history, as a festival day, and its members shall dine together at least once in each year.

Article XV.

LOCAL SECRETARIES.

WHEN ten or more members of this Society shall be resident in a city or town of the State of California, one of their number may be appointed Local Secretary by the Council, to hold office for one year, or until his successor be duly appointed. Subject to the approval of the Council, a Local Secretary may, in conjunction with the members locally resident, organize a Chapter of this Society; arrange local commemorations of men and events of Colonial history; hold annual and special meetings and elect such local officers as may be desired; provided, however, that all reports and recommendations from said Local Chapter to this Society shall be made through said Local Secretary.

Article XVI.

FLAG.

THE Flag of this Society shall be Argent, a Cross of Saint George gules; an escutcheon or, bordered sable, charged with a Grizzly Bear, passant, proper; under the motto "Eureka."

Article XVII.

INSIGNIA AND DIPLOMA.

THE Insignia and Diploma of Membership shall be those of the General Society; provided, however, that members may receive a certificate of membership in this Society, signed by the Governor, Registrar and Secretary, in such form as may be prescribed by the Council

Article XVIII.

SEAL.

THE Great Seal of this society shall be: Within a beaded annulet a title scroll; Society of Colonial Wars in the State of California 1642-1775 surrounding a group of Colo-

nial weapons; over all a shield, Quarterly, I and IV; Gules a tower triple-towered or. (Castile). II and III; Argent a lion rampant gules, crowned or. (Leon). Upon a chief of the last a grizzly bear, passant proper. (California).

Article XIX.

COURTS.

THE General Court of the Society shall be held on "Forefathers' Day," the twenty-first day of December in each year.

Should said date fall on a Sunday, then the General Court shall be held on the following Monday.

Special Courts may be called by the Governor at such times as in his opinion the interests of the Society may demand, and they must be called by the Secretary, by direction of the Council, or upon the written request of nine members.

The notice for the holding of the General Court shall be given as is provided by law for the notice of annual meetings of corporations in the State of California.

All notices of Special Courts shall be sent out at least twenty days before the date of such Courts.

Ten members shall be necessary to constitute a quorum for the transaction of business, and in all cases, except the amendment of the By-Laws, a majority of those present, or represented by proxy shall constitute a vote.

Article XX.

PROXIES AND CUMULATIVE VOTING.

ANY member who is unable to be present at a General or Special Court of this Society may, nevertheless, have his vote counted, having first duly authorized, in writing, a member to act as his proxy thereat.

In all elections of officers, cumulative voting shall be lawful.

Article XXI.

ANCESTRAL RECORD.

EVERY member who shall present to the Registrar, duly verified before an officer authorized by law to administer an oath, a statement in writing, containing the particulars of his marriage, and the names and dates of the birth of his children, and such facts concerning his life and ancestry, and the ancestry of his wife, as he may desire to have perpetuated, shall be entitled to have the same filed among the archives, and spread at large upon the records of the Registrar of this Society.

Article XXII.

ADDRESSES OF MEMBERS.

IT shall be the duty of every member to inform the Secretary, by written communication, of his place of residence, and of any change thereof, and of his postoffice address. Service of any notice under the By-Laws on any member, addressed to his last residence or postoffice address, forwarded by mail, shall be sufficient service of notice.

Article XXIII.

DECEASE OF MEMBERS.

UPON the death of any member, notice thereof, and of the time and place of the funeral, shall be sent by the Secretary to every member residing in the county of the deceased member, and thereupon it shall become the duty of members, if practicable, to attend the obsequies.

Upon the information of the decease of a member, the Governor shall appoint from the Society four members as a Committee to represent the Society at the funeral.

Any member who becomes aware of the death of a fellow member, shall immediately notify the Secretary of the fact.

Article XXIV.

FEES AND DUES.

THE initiation fee shall be ten dollars. The annual dues shall be five dollars, payable between the first days of January and March of each year, after which latter date members who have not paid will be debarred from voting at the meetings of the Society; *provided*, that any member elected during the last three months of the year shall not be required to pay the annual dues for the year next ensuing. The payment at any one time of fifty dollars, in addition to the initiation fee, shall constitute life membership, such payment being in lieu of all annual dues. When the number of life members shall reach one hundred, the fee for life membership thereafter shall be one hundred dollars.

Any of the Charter members of this Society who, on the 30th day of November, 1895, was a member of another State Society, and who shall desire to retain his older membership, is hereby declared to be a member of this Society, with power to vote at any of its meetings, and eligible to any of its offices, and he shall be exempt from the payment of annual dues so long as he shall retain his membership in his former Society, and pay annual dues therein.

Any member who may contribute two hundred and fifty dollars to the "Permanent Fund" of the Society, shall be exempt from payment of all annual dues, and this exemption shall extend in perpetuity to his lineal successors in membership from the same propositus, one at a time, who shall be selected for such exemption by the Society, said perpetual membership to be transmitted by the holder subject to the approval of the Council.

The Council shall have the power to drop from the roll the name of any member who shall be at least two years in arrears for dues, and shall fail on proper notice to pay the same within sixty days; and on being dropped his membership shall cease, but he may be restored to membership at any time by the Council upon his written application and the payment of all arrears to the date of his restoration.

Article XXV.
PERMANENT FUND.

THERE shall be a "Permanent Fund," to be derived from all Life Membership fees and contributions, to remain forever for the use of the Society, the income only of which shall be expended.

Article XXVI.
GOVERNOR.

THE Governor, or in his absence the Deputy-Governor or Lieutenant-Governor, or a Chairman *pro tempore*, shall preside at all Courts of the Society, and shall exercise the duties of a presiding officer, under parliamentary rules, subject to an appeal to the Society. He shall be a member *ex officio* of all Committees, except Nominating Committees, and the Committee on Membership.

The Governor shall shall have power to convene the Council at his discretion.

Article XXVII.
SECRETARY.

THE Secretary shall conduct the general correspondence of the Society, and keep a record thereof. He shall notify all persons elected to membership in the Society, and shall perform such other duties as the Society or his office may require. He shall have charge of the seal, certificates of incorporation, books, by-laws, historical and other documents and records of the Society, other than those required to be deposited with the Registrar. He shall notify the Registrar of all admissions to membership. He shall certify all acts of the Society and, when required, authenticate them under seal.

He shall have charge of the printing and of publications issued by the Society. He shall give due notice of the time and place of holding all Courts of the Society and of the meetings of the Council. He shall be *ex officio* Secretary of the Council, and he shall keep a full and complete record of all the proceedings and orders of the Society and of the Council. In his absence from any meeting a Secretary *pro tempore* may be designated therefor.

The Secretary may be paid a salary at the discretion of the Council.

Article XXVIII.
TREASURER.

THE Treasurer shall collect and keep the funds and securities of the Society. The money of the Society shall be deposited in some bank in the city of residence of the Treasurer to the credit of the "Society of Colonial Wars in the State of California," and such money shall be drawn thence on the checks of the Treasurer for the purposes of the Society only. He shall keep a true account of his receipts and payments, and at each annual meeting render the same to the Society.

For the faithful performance of his duty he may be required to give such security as the Council deems proper.

Article XXIX.
HISTORIAN.

THE Historian shall keep a detailed record of all historical and commemorative celebrations of the Society, and shall edit and prepare for publication such historical addresses, papers and other documents as the Council may see proper to publish.

He shall also prepare a necrological list for the year, with biographies of deceased members, and cause the same to be printed in an appropriate form, by direction of the Council.

Article XXX.

RESISTRAR.

THE Registrar shall receive and file all the proofs upon which membership or supplemental ancestral record has been granted, and record a short abstract thereof. He shall make a record of all diplomas countersigned by him, and of all documents which the Society may obtain; and, under the direction of the Council, he shall make copies of such papers as the owners may not be willing to have in the keeping of the Society.

Article XXXI.

CHANCELLOR

THE Chancellor shall be a lawyer, duly admitted to the bar, and it shall be his duty to give legal opinions on matters affecting the Society when demanded by proper authority.

Article XXXII.

SURGEON.

THE Surgeon shall be a practicing physician.

Article XXXIII.

CHAPLAIN.

THE Chaplain shall be an ordained minister of a Christian church, and it shall be his duty to officiate when called upon by the proper officers.

Article XXXIV.

ORDER OF BUSINESS.

THE General and Special Courts of the Society shall be conducted according to parliamentary law, and the following order of business shall be followed so far the same may be applicable:

1. Calling the Court to order by the Governor.
2. Prayer by the Chaplain.
3. Reading of the record of prior Courts not acted upon.
4. Reports from Officers, Council and Committees.
5. Unfinished business.
6. New business.
7. Elections.
8. Benediction by the Chaplain.

Article XXXV.

AMENDMENTS.

NO alteration or amendment of these by-laws shall be made unless notice thereof shall be duly given in writing, signed by the member proposing the same, at a General or Special Court of the Society, nor unless the same shall be adopted at a subsequent Court, held at least thirty days after such notice, by a vote of two-thirds of the members present.

Society of Colonial Wars
In the
State of California

Instituted November 30, 1895
Chartered December 19, 1895

Society of Colonial Wars
in the
State of California.

Officers,
Gentlemen of the Council and
Standing Committees.
1897.

GOVERNOR,
HOLDRIDGE OZRO COLLINS,
Los Angeles.

DEPUTY GOVERNOR,
HON. ERSKINE MAYO ROSS.

LIEUTENANT GOVERNOR,
SPENCER ROANE THORPE.

SECRETARY,
CHARLES PUTNAM FENNER,
930 S. Flower St., Los Angeles.

TREASURER,
FRANK PUTNAM FLINT,
First and Spring Sts., Los Angeles.

REGISTRAR,
EDWARD THOMAS HARDEN,
2331 Thompson St., Los Angeles.

HISTORIAN,
BRADNER WELLS LEE.

CHANCELLOR,
GEORGE JULES DENIS.

SURGEON,
JOHN RANDOLPH HAYNES, M. D.

CHAPLAIN,
REV. ALEXANDER MOSS MERWIN.

GENTLEMEN OF THE COUNCIL.

Spencer Roane Thorpe, *Chairman.*
Rev. William Augustus Brewer.
Hon. Elisha Williams McKinstry.
Motley Hewes Flint.
Henry Atherton Nichols.
Willard Atherton Nichols.
Frank Clarke Prescott.
John Kennedy Stout.
Andrew Roane Thorpe.
Hon. Cameron Erskine Thom.

COMMITTEE ON MEMBERSHIP.

George Jules Denis.
Frank Putnam Flint.
Spencer Roane Thorpe.
Bradner Wells Lee.
John Randolph Haynes, M. D.

COMMITTEE ON HISTORICAL DOCUMENTS.

Bradner Wells Lee, *Chairman Ex-Officio.*
John Randolph Haynes, M. D.
Prof. Edward Singleton Holden.
Rev. Alexander Moss Merwin.

COMMITTEE ON ENTERTAINMENT.

George Jules Denis.
Frank Putnam Flint.
Edward Thomas Harden.
Frank Clarke Prescott.
John Randolph Haynes, M. D.

DELEGATES TO THE GENERAL SOCIETY.

Motley Hewes Flint.
Prof. Edward Singleton Holden.
George Timothy Kline.
Hon. Elisha Williams McKinstry.
Capt. Albert Henry Payson.

ALTERNATES.

Lieut.-Col. William Anthony Elderkin, U. S. A.
Allen Lysander Colton.
William Marcy Klink.
William Hammond Wright.
John Kennedy Stout.

DEPUTY GOVERNOR GENERAL.

Spencer Roane Thorpe.

Membership Roll.

BREWER, REV. WILLIAM AUGUSTUS, Clergyman, - San Mateo.
COLLINS, HOLDRIDGE OZRO, Lawyer, - - - - Los Angeles.
COLTON, PROF. ALLEN LYSANDER, Astronomer, Lick Observatory.
DENIS, GEORGE JULES, United States District Attorney, Los Angeles.
ELDERKIN, LIEUT.-COL. WILLIAM ANTHONY, U.S.A., Chicago, Ill.
FENNER, CHARLES PUTNAM, Journalist, - - - Los Angeles.
FLINT, FRANK PUTNAM, Lawyer, - - - - - Los Angeles.
FLINT, MOTLEY HEWES, Postoffice Inspector, - - Los Angeles.
HARDEN, EDWARD THOMAS, Electrician, - - - Los Angeles.
HAYNES, JOHN RANDOLPH, M. D., Physician, - - Los Angeles.
HOLDEN, PROF. EDWARD SINGLETON, Astronomer, Lick Observatory.
KLINE, GEORGE TIMOTHY, Auditor S. P. Co., - - San Francisco.
KLINE, WILLIAM MARCY, Accountant, - - - San Francisco.
LEE, BRADNER WELLS, Lawyer, - - - - - Los Angeles.
MERWIN, REV. ALEXANDER MOSS, Clergyman, - Pasadena, Cal.
McKINSTRY, HON. ELISHA WILLIAMS,
    Ex-Justice Supreme Court, Lawyer, San Francisco.
NICHOLS, HENRY ATHERTON, Rancher, - - - - Redlands.
NICHOLS, WILLARD ATHERTON, Civil Engineer, - - Redlands.
PAYSON, CAPT. ALBERT HENRY, Civil Engineer, - - San Mateo.
PRESCOTT, FRANK CLARKE, Lawyer, - - - - Redlands.
ROSS, HON. ERSKINE MAYO, United States Circuit Judge, Los Angeles.
STOUT, JOHN KENNEDY, Lawyer, - - - - Spokane, Wash.
THOM, HON. CAMERON ERSKINE, Lawyer, ex-Mayor, Los Angeles.
THORPE, ANDREW ROANE, Dentist, - - - - - Los Angeles.
THORPE, SPENCER ROANE, Rancher, - - - - Los Angeles.
WRIGHT, WM. HAMMOND, Astronomer, - - Williams Bay, Wis.

Society of Colonial Wars
in the State of California.

Instituted at Los Angeles, November 30, 1895.
Chartered by the General Society, December 19, 1895.

**Officers,
Gentlemen of the Council and
Standing Committees.
1898.**

GOVERNOR,
HOLDRIDGE OZRO COLLINS,
Los Angeles.

DEPUTY GOVERNOR,
HON. ERSKINE MAYO ROSS.

LIEUTENANT GOVERNOR,
SPENCER ROANE THORPE.

SECRETARY,
CHARLES PUTNAM FENNER,
930 S. Flower St., Los Angeles.

TREASURER,
FRANK PUTNAM FLINT.

REGISTRAR,
EDWARD THOMAS HARDEN,
2331 Thompson St., Los Angeles.

HISTORIAN,
BRADNER WELLS LEE.

CHANCELLOR,
GEORGE JULES DENIS.

SURGEON,
JOHN RANDOLPH HAYNES, M. D.

CHAPLAIN,
REV. ALEXANDER MOSS MERWIN.

GENTLEMEN OF THE COUNCIL.

HARRISON BABCOCK ALEXANDER,
    MOTLEY HEWES FLINT,
        HON. GEORGE ELI HALL,
HON. ELISHA WILLIAMS MCKINSTRY,
    WILLARD ATHERTON NICHOLS,
        ISAAC HILLIARD POLK,
FRANK CLARKE PRESCOTT,
    FREDERICK HASTINGS RINDGE,
        HON. CAMERON ERSKINE THOM.

COMMITTEE ON MEMBERSHIP.

GEORGE JULES DENIS,
    FRANK PUTNAM FLINT,
        EDWARD THOMAS HARDEN,
            BRADNER WELLS LEE,
                SPENCER ROANE THORPE.

COMMITTEE ON HISTORICAL DOCUMENTS.

BRADNER WELLS LEE, *Chairman Ex-Officio*,
    REV. ALFRED LEE BREWER, D. D.,
        PHILIP KING BROWN, M. D.,
            MILLARD TRACY HARTSON.

COMMITTEE ON ENTERTAINMENT.

GEORGE JULES DENIS,
    CHARLES PUTNAM FENNER,
        FRANK PUTNAM FLINT,
            JOHN RANDOLPH HAYNES, M. D.,
                FRANK CLARKE PRESCOTT.

DELEGATES TO THE GENERAL SOCIETY.

REV. WILLIAM AUGUSTUS BREWER,
    GEORGE TIMOTHY KLINK,
        HENRY ATHERTON NICHOLS,
            CAPTAIN ALBERT HENRY PAYSON,
                JOHN KENNEDY STOUT.

ALTERNATES.

ASAHEL GEORGE AVERY,
    EDWIN RODOLPH DIMOND,
        LIEUT.-COL. WILLIAM ANTHONY ELDERKIN, U. S. A.
            FREDERICK SCHANDER MOODY,
    LIEUT.-COMMANDER JOSIAH RUMBALL STANTON, U. S. N.

DEPUTY GOVERNOR GENERAL.
    SPENCER ROANE THORPE.

Roll of Members.

ALEXANDER, HARRISON BABCOCK, Lawyer,	San Gabriel
AVERY, ASAHEL GEORGE, Lawyer, Corporation Counsel,	Spokane, Wash.
BREWER, REV. ALFRED LEE, Clergyman,	San Mateo.
BREWER, REV. WILLIAM AUGUSTUS, Clergyman,	San Mateo.
BROWN, PHILIP KING, M. D., Physician	San Francisco.
COLLINS, LIEUT. CHARLES LEE, U. S. Army,	Whipple, Arizona.
COLLINS, HOLDRIDGE OZRO, Lawyer,	Los Angeles.
DARNEAL, HERVEY, Law Reporter,	Alameda.
DENIS, GEORGE JULES, Lawyer,	Los Angeles.
DIMOND, EDWIN RODOLPH, Merchant,	San Francisco.
DOOLITTLE, GEORGE TILTON, M. D., Physician,	Spokane, Wash.
ELDERKIN, LIEUT.-COL. WILLIAM ANTHONY, U. S. Army,	Chicago, Ill.
FENNER, CHARLES PUTNAM, Accountant,	Los Angeles.
FLINT, FRANK PUTNAM, U. S. District Attorney,	Los Angeles.
FLINT, MOTLEY HEWES, U. S. Post Office Inspector,	Los Angeles.
HALL, CHARLES LANDER, Trader,	St. Michaels, Alaska.
HALL, HON. GEORGE ELI, Turkish Consul General, etc.,	San Francisco.
HARDEN, EDWARD THOMAS, Electrician,	Los Angeles.
HARTSON, MILLARD TRACY, Lawyer,	Spokane, Wash.
HAWLEY, WALTER AUGUSTUS, Merchant,	Santa Barbara.
HAYNES, JOHN RANDOLPH, M. D., Physician,	Los Angeles.
KLINK, GEORGE TIMOTHY, Auditor Southern Pacific Co.,	San Francisco.
KLINK, WILLIAM MARCY, Accountant,	San Francisco.
LEE, BRADNER WELLS, Lawyer,	Los Angeles.
McKINSTRY, HON. ELISHA WILLIAMS, Lawyer,	San Francisco.
Ex-Justice Supreme Court of California.	
MERWIN, REV. ALEXANDER MOSS, Clergyman,	Pasadena.
MOODY, FREDERICK SCHANDER, Merchant,	San Francisco.
NICHOLS, HENRY ATHERTON, Fruit Grower,	Redlands.
NICHOLS, WILLARD ATHERTON, Civil Engineer,	Redlands.
OSGOOD, JOSIAH ALONZO, Civil and Mechanical Engineer,	Los Angeles.
PAYSON, CAPT. ALBERT HENRY, Civil Engineer,	San Mateo.
POLK, ISAAC HILLIARD, Miner,	Los Angeles.
POST, FRANK TRUMAN, Lawyer,	Spokane, Wash.
PRESCOTT, FRANK CLARKE, Lawyer,	Redlands.
RINDGE, FREDERICK HASTINGS, Manufacturer,	Santa Monica.
ROSS, HON. ERSKINE MAYO, U. S. Circuit Judge,	Los Angeles.
STANTON, LIEUT.-COMMANDER JOSIAH RUMBALL, U. S. Navy,	Mare Island.
STOUT, JOHN KENNEDY, Lawyer,	Spokane, Wash.
THOM, HON. CAMERON ERSKINE, Lawyer,	Los Angeles.
THORPE, SPENCER ROANE, Rancher,	Los Angeles.
WRIGHT, WILLIAM HAMMOND, Astronomer,	Mt. Hamilton.

San Francisco Chapter
of the
Society of Colonial Wars
in the
State of California.

LOCAL SECRETARY,
Hon. George Eli Hall,
Parrott Building.

The San Francisco Chapter was organized on February 3, 1898, under the provisions of Article XV of the State Society By-Laws. "Members of the California State Society residing within a radius of fifty miles of San Francisco shall be eligible for membership in this Chapter."

**Officers and Committees,
1898.**

PRESIDENT,
Hon. Elisha Williams McKinstry.

VICE-PRESIDENT,
Captain Albert Henry Payson.

LOCAL SECRETARY AND EX-OFFICIO TREASURER,
Hon. George Eli Hall.

COMMITTEE ON MEMBERSHIP,
Philip King Brown, M. D.,
George Timothy Klink.

COMMITTEE ON ENTERTAINMENT,
Rev. William Augustus Brewer,
Frederick Schander Moody.

Flag of the Society of Colonial Wars
In the State of California

Society of Colonial Wars

in the

State of California

Instituted at Los Angeles, November 30, 1893.
Chartered by the General Society, December 19, 1893.

Officers.
Gentlemen of the Council and
Standing Committees.
1899.

GOVERNOR,
HOLDRIDGE OZRO COLLINS,
Los Angeles.

DEPUTY GOVERNOR,
HON. ERSKINE MAYO ROSS.

LIEUTENANT GOVERNOR,
SPENCER ROANE THORPE.

SECRETARY AND TREASURER,
HARRISON BABCOCK ALEXANDER,
Room 420 Henne Block, Los Angeles.

REGISTRAR,
EDWARD THOMAS HARDEN,
2331 Thompson St., Los Angeles.

HISTORIAN,
BRADNER WELLS LEE.

CHANCELLOR,
GEORGE JULES DENIS.

SURGEON,
JOHN RANDOLPH HAYNES, M. D.

CHAPLAIN,
REV. ALEXANDER MOSS MERWIN.

DEPUTY GOVERNOR GENERAL,
SPENCER ROANE THORPE,
Los Angeles.

GENTLEMEN OF THE COUNCIL,

FOR ONE YEAR.

Motley Hewes Flint,
　　　Frank Clarke Prescott,
　　　　　　Isaac Hilliard Polk.

FOR TWO YEARS.

Hon. Elisha Williams McKinstry,
　　　Frederick Hastings Rindge,
　　　　　　Willard Atherton Nichols.

FOR THREE YEARS.

Hon. Cameron Erskine Thom,
　　　Captain Josiah Alonzo Osgood,
　　　　　　Hon. George Eli Hall.

COMMITTEE ON MEMBERSHIP,

George Jules Denis,
　　　Frank Putnam Flint,
　　　　　Edward Thomas Harden,
　　　　　　Bradner Wells Lee,
　　　　　　　Spencer Roane Thorpe.

COMMITTEE ON HISTORICAL DOCUMENTS,

Bradner Wells Lee, *Chairman Ex-Officio,*
　　　Rev. Alfred Lee Brewer, D. D.
　　　　　Philip King Brown, M. D.,
　　　　　　Walter Augustus Hawley.

COMMITTEE ON ENTERTAINMENT,

George Jules Denis,
　　　Charles Putnam Fenner,
　　　　　Frank Putnam Flint,
　　　　　　John Randolph Haynes, M. D.,
　　　　　　　Frank Clarke Prescott.

DELEGATES TO THE GENERAL SOCIETY,

Rev. William Augustus Brewer,
　　　George Timothy Klink,
　　　　　Frederick Hastings Rindge,
　　　　　　Captain Albert Henry Payson,
　　　　　　　Holdridge Ozro Collins.

ALTERNATES,

Edwin Rodolph Dimond,
　　　Hon. George Eli Hall,
　　　　　Frederick Schander Moody,
　　　　　　Henry Atherton Nichols,
Lieut.-Commander Josiah Rumball Stanton, U. S. N.

Roll of Members.

ALEXANDER, HARRISON BABCOCK, Lawyer,	San Gabriel
BREWER, REV. ALFRED LEE, D. D., Clergyman	San Mateo
BREWER, REV. WILLIAM AUGUSTUS, Clergyman,	San Mateo
BROWN, PHILIP KING, M. D., Physician,	San Francisco
COLLINS, CAPTAIN CHARLES LEE, U. S. A., Legation U.S.,	Caracas Venezuela
COLLINS, HOLDRIDGE OZRO, Lawyer,	Los Angeles
DARNEAL, HERVEY, Law Reporter,	Alameda
DENIS, GEORGE JULES, Lawyer,	Los Angeles
DIMOND, EDWIN RODOLPH, Merchant,	San Francisco
ELDERKIN, COLONEL WILLIAM ANTHONY, U. S. Army,	Chicago, Ill.
FENNER, CHARLES PUTNAM, Accountant,	Los Angeles
FLINT, FRANK PUTNAM, U. S. District Attorney,	Los Angeles
FLINT, MOTLEY HEWES, U. S. Post Office Inspector,	Los Angeles
HALL, CHARLES LANDER, Trader,	St. Michaels, Alaska
HALL, HON. GEORGE ELI, Turkish Consul General, etc.,	San Francisco
HARDEN, EDWARD THOMAS, Electrician,	Los Angeles
HAWLEY, WALTER AUGUSTUS, Merchant,	Santa Barbara
HAYNES, JOHN RANDOLPH, M. D., Physician,	Los Angeles
KLINK, GEORGE TIMOTHY, Auditor Southern Pacific Co.,	San Francisco
KLINK, WILLIAM MARCY, Accountant,	San Francisco
LEE, BRADNER WELLS, Lawyer,	Los Angeles
McKINSTRY, HON. ELISHA WILLIAMS, Lawyer,	San Francisco
Ex-Justice Supreme Court of California.	
MERWIN, REV. ALEXANDER MOSS, Clergyman,	Pasadena
MOODY, FREDERICK SCHANDER, Merchant,	San Francisco
NICHOLS, HENRY ATHERTON, Banker,	Cambridge, Mass.
NICHOLS, WILLARD ATHERTON, Civil Engineer,	Redlands
OSGOOD, JOSIAH ALONZO, Civil and Mechanical Engineer,	Los Angeles
PAYSON, CAPT. ALBERT HENRY, Civil Engineer,	San Mateo
POLK, ISAAC HILLIARD, Miner,	Los Angeles
PRESCOTT, FRANK CLARKE, Lawyer,	Redlands
RINDGE, FREDERICK HASTINGS, Manufacturer,	Santa Monica
ROSS, HON. ERSKINE MAYO, U. S. Circuit Judge,	Los Angeles
STANTON, LIEUT.-COMMANDER JOSIAH RUMBALL, U. S. Navy,	Mare Island
THOM, HON. CAMERON ERSKINE, Lawyer,	Los Angeles
THOM, CATESBY CHARLES, Sergt. Battery D, Cal. H. A.,	Manila, Philippines
THOM, CAMERON DeHART, Sergt. Battery D, Cal. H. A.,	Manila, Philippines
THORPE, SPENCER ROANE, Rancher,	Los Angeles
WRIGHT, WILLIAM HAMMOND, Astronomer,	Mt. Hamilton

San Francisco Chapter
of the
Society of Colonial Wars
in the
State of California.

LOCAL SECRETARY.
Hon. George Eli Hall,
Parrott Building.

The San Francisco Chapter was organized on February 3, 1898, under the provisions of Article XV of the State Society By-Laws. "Members of the California State Society residing within a radius of fifty miles of San Francisco shall be eligible for membership in this Chapter."

Officers and Committees.
1899.

PRESIDENT,
Rev. Alfred Lee Brewer, D. D.

VICE PRESIDENT,
Edwin Rodolph Dimond.

SECRETARY-TREASURER,
Hon. George Eli Hall.

COMMITTEE ON MEMBERSHIP,
Philip King Brown, M. D.
George Timothy Klink.

COMMITTEE ON ENTERTAINMENT,
Rev. William Augustus Brewer,
Frederick Schander Moody.

... By=Laws ...

Article XV.
Local Secretaries.

WHEN ten or more members of this Society shall be resident in a city or town of the State of California, one of their number may be appointed Local Secretary by the Council, to hold office for one year, or until his successor be duly appointed. Subject to the approval of the Council, a Local Secretary may, in conjunction with the members locally resident, organize a Chapter of this Society; arrange local commemorations of men and events of Colonial history; hold annual and special meetings and elect such local officers as may be desired; provided, however, that all reports and recommendations from said Local Chapter to this Society shall be made through said Local Secretary.

The following amendment to Article VI was adopted by the Fourth General Court, viz:

At the Election of 1898, three Gentlemen of the Council shall be elected for a term of one year, three for a term of two years, and three for a term of three years, and thereafter at each election, three Gentlemen of the Council shall be elected for a term of three years.

Greeting

To Our Members!

The New Year commences with happy auspices for the prosperity of the Society of Colonial Wars in the State of California.

A satisfactory Treasury, and the enthusiastic loyalty of the gentlemen associated in this organization, are an assurance to those who founded this Society, that their efforts to establish a permanent integral unit of the General Society were not in vain.

Since our Third General Court another Society on the Pacific Coast has been received into the Union. On November 16, 1898, a Charter was granted to a Society in the State of Washington, instituted at Spokane, with the Honorable John Kennedy Stout as Governor. We extend to the gentlemen of that Society our congratulations and most cordial well-wishes for their success. Five of those gentlemen were our fellow members up to the convening of our last General Court, when they withdrew from us feeling that their adherence was due to their home Society.

We take great pride in the very honorable record of this Society in the war with Spain. We gave seven of our members to the service of the Government in that contest, to-wit:

Colonel William Anthony Elderkin of the Commissary Department, and

Captain Charles Lee Collins, Eleventh Infantry, both of the regular Army.

Lieutenant Commander Josiah Rumball Stanton, of the Navy.

Major Frank Clarke Prescott, and

First Lieutenant Charles Putnam Fenner, of the Seventh Regiment Infantry, California Volunteers.

Sergeant Cameron DeBart Thom, and

Sergeant Catesby Charles Thom, of Battery D, California Heavy Artillery. These last named, Thom brothers, are now serving with their Command at Manila. May they both come home with straps on their shoulders and commissions in their pockets.

Only three of our members have neglected to send their photographs and biographies and our records in this behalf are very satisfactory. The Society Album is a very attractive feature in our Library. It is hoped that during the coming year the Council will feel justified in ordering the publication of the Society Book, for which many are looking with expectation.

At our Fourth General Court, an amendment to Article VI of the By-Laws was adopted, making the term of office of the Gentlemen of the Council three years, and providing for the election of three members every year, leaving six members to hold over.

The Second General Assembly will be held at Baltimore, Maryland, in May, 1899. As the General Assembly meets only triennially, matters of importance to the welfare of all the State Societies will be discussed, and we hope to be represented on that occasion by some of our Delegates or Alternates.

With the heartiest wishes for a Happy New Year to you all and an expression of my profound appreciation of the honors conferred upon myself,

    I subscribe myself

        Very sincerely your servant,

                Holdridge Ozro Collins,

Los Angeles,   Governor.
   January 2, 1899.

"SOCIETAS PIA MAJORUM VENERATIONE
CONDITA IN AETERNUM FLOREAT"

Flag of the Society of Colonial Wars.

OFFICE OF THE GOVERNOR

It is my mournful duty to announce the death, at San Mateo, on February 16, 1899, of

Rev. Alfred Lee Brewer, D. D.

one of the most beloved members of this Society and the President of the San Francisco Chapter.

I have appointed Hon. George E. Hall, Captain Albert H. Payson, Frederick S. Moody, George T. Klink and Philip K. Brown, M. D. the Committee to represent this Society at the funeral.

HOLDRIDGE OZRO COLLINS,
Governor.

OFFICE OF THE GOVERNOR

At the Island of Cebu, on September 7, 1899, departed this life

Charles Lee Collins

Captain in the Twenty-third Regiment of Infantry, United States Army.

Captain Collins was graduated from the United States Military Academy at West Point, in 1882, and commissioned a Second Lieutenant of infantry, from which time up to his death he was in active service on the frontier and in staff details.

In the winter of 1898, while First Lieutenant and Adjutant of the Eleventh Infantry, he was ordered to Caracas, Venezuela, as Military Attache of the United States Legation. He remained at this place over a year, discharging the duties of this position in a manner so satisfac-

tory to the government of Venezuela that he was decorated with the famous "Order of the Liberator" (Busto de Bolivar).

In July, 1899, he sailed from San Francisco upon the U. S. transport 'Ohio" in command of recruits for the Philippine Islands, and very soon after reaching Cebu, he died from the effects of a surgical operation.

Captain Collins was one of the incorporators and the first Secretary of the California Society of Sons of the Revolution, and he was elected to membership in this Society on November 4, 1897. In right of his father he was a companion of the Military Order of the Loyal Legion, and by representation, a member of the Pennsylvania Society of the War of 1812.

He leaves a widow, Emma Byrd Beach Collins, but no children.

The San Francisco Chapter is requested to represent this Society, and to extend all possible assistance to those having charge of the remains upon their arrival at San Francisco.

HOLDRIDGE OZRO COLLINS,
Governor.

Los Angeles,
    September 18, 1899.

La Ciudad de Nuestra Señora la Reina de Los Angeles

William Hammond Wright

Society of Colonial Wars
in the State of California

Instituted at Los Angeles, November 30, 1895.
Chartered by the General Society, December 19, 1895.

Officers,
Gentlemen of the Council and
Standing Committees.
1900.

GOVERNOR,
HOLDRIDGE OZRO COLLINS,
Los Angeles.

DEPUTY GOVERNOR,
HON. ERSKINE MAYO ROSS.

LIEUTENANT GOVERNOR,
SPENCER ROANE THORPE.

SECRETARY AND TREASURER,
HARRISON BABCOCK ALEXANDER,
Room 420 Henne Block, Los Angeles.

REGISTRAR,
EDWARD THOMAS HARDEN,
2331 Thompson St., Los Angeles.

HISTORIAN,
BRADNER WELLS LEE.

CHANCELLOR,
GEORGE JULES DENIS.

SURGEON,
JOHN RANDOLPH HAYNES, M. D.

CHAPLAIN,
REV. ALEXANDER MOSS MERWIN.

GENTLEMEN OF THE COUNCIL,

Term Expiring 1900.

HON. ELISHA WILLIAMS MCKINSTRY,
    FREDERICK HASTINGS RINDGE,
        WILLARD ATHERTON NICHOLS.

Term Expiring 1901.

HON. CAMERON ERSKINE THOM,
    CAPTAIN JOSIAH ALONZO OSGOOD,
        HON. GEORGE ELI HALL.

Term Expiring 1902.

FRANK PUTNAM FLINT,
    ISAAC HILLIARD POLK,
        CAMERON DEHART THOM.

COMMITTEE ON MEMBERSHIP,

GEORGE JULES DENIS,
    FRANK PUTNAM FLINT,
        EDWARD THOMAS HARDEN,
            BRADNER WELLS LEE,
                SPENCER ROANE THORPE.

COMMITTEE ON HISTORICAL DOCUMENTS,

BRADNER WELLS LEE, *Chairman Ex-Officio*,
    PHILIP KING BROWN, M. D.,
        WALTER AUGUSTUS HAWLEY,
            WILLIAM HAMMOND WRIGHT.

COMMITTEE ON ENTERTAINMENT,

CAPTAIN JOSIAH ALONZO OSGOOD,
    GEORGE JULES DENIS,
        HERVEY DARNEAL,
            JOHN RANDOLPH HAYNES, M. D.,
                MOTLEY HEWES FLINT.

DELEGATES TO THE GENERAL SOCIETY,

REV. WILLIAM AUGUSTUS BREWER,
    GEORGE TIMOTHY KLINK,
        FREDERICK HASTINGS RINDGE,
            CAPTAIN ALBERT HENRY PAYSON,
                HOLDRIDGE OZRO COLLINS.

ALTERNATES,

EDWIN RODOLPH DIMOND,
    HON. GEORGE ELI HALL,
        FREDERICK SCHANDER MOODY,
            HENRY ATHERTON NICHOLS,
                COMMANDER JOSIAH RUMBALL STANTON, U. S. N.

DEPUTY GOVERNOR GENERAL,

SPENCER ROANE THORPE.

Insignia of the
Society of Colonial Wars.

Roll of Members

ALEXANDER, HARRISON BABCOCK, Lawyer,	Los Angeles
BREWER, REV. WILLIAM AUGUSTUS, Clergyman,	San Mateo
BROWN, FRANK LAMPSON, Merchant,	San Francisco
BROWN, PHILIP KING, M. D., Physician,	San Francisco
COLLINS, HOLDRIDGE OZRO, Lawyer,	Los Angeles
COWLES, WILLIAM NORTHROPE, Manufacturer,	San Francisco
DARNEAL, HERVEY, Law Reporter,	Alameda
DENIS, GEORGE JULES, Lawyer,	Los Angeles
DIMOND, EDWIN RODOLPH, Merchant,	San Francisco
FENNER, CHARLES PUTNAM, U. S. Customs Inspector,	Manila, Luzon
FLINT, FRANK PUTNAM, U. S. District Attorney,	Los Angeles
FLINT, MOTLEY HEWES, U. S. Post Office Inspector,	Los Angeles
HALL, CHARLES LANDER, Trader,	St. Michaels, Alaska
HALL, HON. GEORGE ELI, Turkish Consul General, etc.,	San Francisco
HALL, MAURICE ARTHUR, Secretary Turkish Consulate Gen'l,	San Francisco
HARDEN, EDWARD THOMAS, Electrician,	Los Angeles
HAWLEY, WALTER AUGUSTUS, Merchant,	Santa Barbara
HAYNES, JOHN RANDOLPH, M. D., Physician,	Los Angeles
KLINK, GEORGE TIMOTHY, Auditor Southern Pacific Co.,	San Francisco
KLINK, WILLIAM MARCY, Accountant,	San Francisco
LEE, BRADNER WELLS, Lawyer,	Los Angeles
McKINSTRY, HON. ELISHA WILLIAMS, Lawyer, Ex-Justice Supreme Court of California,	San Francisco
MERWIN, REV. ALEXANDER MOSS, Clergyman,	Pasadena
MOODY, FREDERICK SCHANDER, Merchant,	Burlingame
NICHOLS, HENRY ATHERTON, Banker,	Cambridge, Mass.
NICHOLS, WILLARD ATHERTON, Civil Engineer,	Redlands
OSGOOD, JOSIAH ALONZO, Civil and Mechanical Engineer,	Los Angeles
PAYSON, ALBERT HENRY, Civil Engineer,	San Mateo
POLK, ISAAC HILLIARD, Miner,	Los Angeles
PRESCOTT, FRANK CLARKE, Capt. 43d Regt. U. S. V.,	Philippine Islands
RINDGE, FREDERICK HASTINGS, Manufacturer,	Santa Monica
ROSS, HON. ERSKINE MAYO, U. S. Circuit Judge	Los Angeles
STANTON, COMMANDER JOSIAH RUMBALL, U. S. Navy,	Mare Island
THOM, HON. CAMERON ERSKINE,	Los Angeles
THOM, CAMERON DE HART, Rancher,	Glendale
THOM, CATESBY CHARLES, Law Student,	Los Angeles
THORPE, SPENCER ROANE, Rancher,	Los Angeles
WRIGHT, WILLIAM HAMMOND, Astronomer,	Mt. Hamilton

San Francisco Chapter
of the
Society of Colonial Wars
in the
State of California.

LOCAL SECRETARY
PHILIP KING BROWN, M. D.
No. 1220 Sutter Street.

The San Francisco Chapter was organized on February 3, 1898, under the provisions of Article XV of the State Society By-Laws. "Members of the California State Society residing within a radius of fifty miles of San Francisco shall be eligible for membership in this Chapter."

Officers and Committees.
1900.

PRESIDENT,
EDWIN RODOLPH DIMOND.

VICE-PRESIDENT,
HON. GEORGE ELI HALL.

SECRETARY-TREASURER,
PHILIP KING BROWN, M. D.

COMMITTEE ON MEMBERSHIP,
REV. WILLIAM AUGUSTUS BREWER.
GEORGE TIMOTHY KLINK.

COMMITTEE ON ENTERTAINMENT,
FREDERICK SCHANDER MOODY.
CAPTAIN ALBERT HENRY PAYSON.

Seal of the General Society
of Colonial Wars.

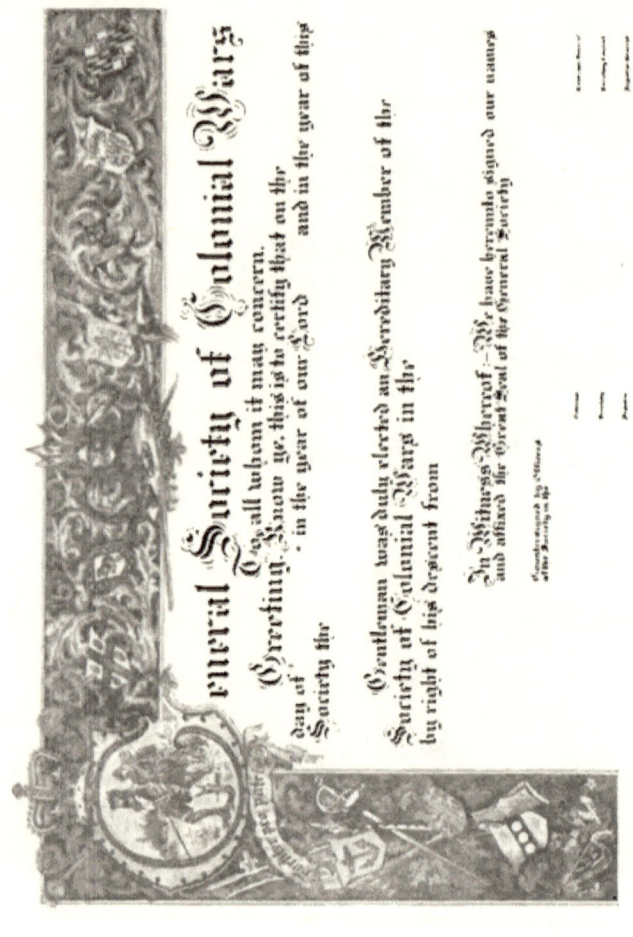

In Memoriam.

Alfred Lee Brewer, D. D.

Born at Norwich, Connecticut, June 4, 1831,
Died at San Mateo, California,
February 16, 1899.

William Anthony Elderkin
Colonel of the United States Army.

Born at Potsdam, New York, May 15, 1839,
Died at Middletown, New York,
January 1, 1900.

Charles Lee Collins
Captain 23rd Infantry, United States Army.

Born at Newport, Kentucky, July 24, 1859,
Died at Cebu, Philippine Islands,
September 7, 1899.

Gentlemen:

At the convening of our Fourth General Court on December 21, 1899, there were thirty-eight gentlemen of this Society. Since that date, Rev. Alfred Lee Brewer, D. D., Colonel William Anthony Elderkin and Captain Charles Lee Collins have died, and we have elected three new members, Frank Lampson Brown, William Northrope Cowles and Maurice Arthur Hall, all of San Francisco, our number remaining unchanged. Since the organization of this Society, we have received into membership fifty gentlemen, and we have lost twelve by death and resignation.

Mr. Fenner has been appointed Inspector of Customs at Manila, Luzon, and Mr. Prescott was commissioned a Captain in the Forty-third Regiment of Infantry, U. S. V., and he is now serving with his Command in the Philippine Islands.

The death of Dr. Brewer, in the midst of his usefulness was a great loss, not only to this Society, but to the State of California, for which he had done so much in the religious and intellectual education of her youth.

The Veteran, William Anthony Elderkin, a Colonel of the United States Army, after a life of valuable service to his country, whose name shines on the roll at Washington, of those who have deserved well of their fellow men, after a prolonged illness, quietly departed from us

> "*Like one who wraps the drapery of his couch
> About him, and lies down to pleasant dreams.*"

The sudden death at Cebu, of Captain Collins, and the almost immediate following of his young widow, were particularly mournful.

We all bow with submission to the fiat that takes from us those who have fulfilled their missions, and who drop from us and their life's earned rewards, like the ripened Autumn leaf; but why, in the eternal economy of human affairs, we should be compelled to suffer the loss of dear friends, relatives and companions, in the flower of their life, whose presence makes existence sweeter to us, who seem to be a necessity in the duties devolving upon them, cut down when the future presents a career of brilliant and honorable usefulness, is a mystery which will never be solved for us this side the Gates of Paradise.

"*I came like water, and like wind I go.*"

We have caused Memorials to the memory of these departed associates, with expressions of profound sympathy for their families, to be spread at large upon our records, that they who, in the coming years shall have charge of this Society, may read the evidence of our esteem for those whose names no longer remain upon our Membership Roll.

Our Annual Roster for 1899 contained the Seal, Vignette and Flag of the California Society, and the Flag of the General Society. With this number we present a fac-simile of the Seal, Insignia and Certificate of Membership which are issued only by the General Society, and the portraits of nearly all of our members. It is hoped that we will be able to obtain engravings of all of the gentlemen composing this Society, for insertion in future publications.

At the Second General Assembly of our Society, held in Baltimore, Maryland, on May 10, 1899, Mr. Frederic J. de Peyster was unanimously re-elected Governor General. It is a matter of congratulation that this gentleman is to continue in the responsible position which he has occupied so satisfactorily to all, since the organization of the Society.

It gives me pleasure to announce the promotion of Mr. Stanton in the Navy, on January 20, 1900, to be Pay Inspector, with the rank of Commander.

Holcombe Ogden Collins
Governor.

Los Angeles,
March 1, 1900.

"GENUS ET PROAVOS ET QUAE NON FECIMUS IPSI
VIX EA NOSTRA VOCO."

THE LATE
ALFRED LEE BREWER, D.D.

Colonel William Anthony Elderkin
(DECEASED)

Captain Charles Lee Collins
(DECEASED)

Harry Woodville Latham
(DECEASED)

Harrison Babcock Alexander

Rev. William Augustus Brewer

Frank Campson Brown

Philip King Brown, M. D.

George Jules Denis

VIRU
FILIA

Frank Putnam Flint

Motley Hewes Flint

Hon. George Eli Hall

Edward Thomas Harden

Walter Augustus Hawley

John Randolph Haynes, M. D.

George Timothy Klink

Bradner Wells Lee

Hon. Elisha Williams McKinstry

Rev. Alexander Moss Merwin

Henry Atherton Nichols

Willard Atherton Nichols

Josiah Alonzo Osgood

Albert Henry Payson

Isaac Hilliard Polk

Captain Frank Clarke Prescott

Frederick Hastings Rindge

Hon. Erskine Mayo Ross

Josiah Rumball Stanton, U. S. N.

Hon. Cameron Erskine Thom

Cameron De Hart Thom
Catesby Charles Thom

Spencer Roane Thorpe

A Vision of St. Nicholas

A Vision of St. Nicholas

Affectionately inscribed to my friend

George Jules Denis

and the

"Placens Uxor"

in memory of the fair Goddess Nicotina,
in whose worship we have joined under the
hospitable umbrage of Bonnie Brae.

Holdridge Ozro Collins,

Los Angeles, California,
Xmas, 1898.

A Christmas Reverie

BY

Holdridge Ozro Collins

In my study, retired from the world's busy jar,
    All forgetful of Courts, and of clients' loud din,
In the delicate fumes from my fragrant cigar,
    To my wonder I see a new era begin.

Old Saint Nicholas enters: his generous back
    Bears a burden of snow from the fierce wintry air,
And while vainly I look for his wonderful pack,
    He possesses himself of my sole easy chair.

As more closely I look at my visitor's face,
    Some unusual frowns of displeasure appear.
"Sir!" I cry, "without doubt, yonder distant cold place
    Is too far from the fire: be at home! Pray draw near."

With a sigh, so profound, that in trouble I start
    Lest my guest may be ill,—for I well knew his worth—
From the depths of his tender and generous heart,
    This reproachful complaint, 'midst his tears issued forth.

"My grateful yearly task is done.
Before the morrow's cheerful sun
Shall ope the portals of the day,
Far must I take my lonely way.
I've left some slight remembrance here,—
Will bring perchance a smile or tear:
But tears not mixed with grief or pain,—
From hearts that wish me come again.
My steeds, discharg'd their varied store,
Impatient wait me at your door.
But ere I urge them in their flight
Across the trackless wastes of night,
One plaint I make,—and make in vain,
But who their deepest sorrows can restrain?"

What my guest in dejection, so sadly had said,
Filled my soul with unutt'rable feelings of dread.
"My dear sir," I remarked, "will you please to explain
The unfortunate cause of your harrowing pain.
Grave indeed must have been mortal's cruel offense,
That can thus such a kind benefactor incense."

    "Alas," he said, "for many years
     I've had my constant growing fears
     That all my care has been in vain,
     To stretch the limit of my reign.
     When e'er upon this annual eve
     The portals of my home I leave,
     Beneath my seat the yearly hoard
     Of curious treasures safely stored,
     One solace of my flight I miss,—
     My joy and comfort. See, 'tis this."

On his small meerschaum Pipe there displayed to my view,
An inquisitive glance, in my wonder, I threw.
At the sight, in amazement, "Good heavens!" I shout,
"Why, dear sir, your most ven'rable Pipe has gone out."
In confusion I stood, and unable to guess
What the omen might mean; and unwilling to press
My companion its import concealed to explain,
Lest perchance I'd offend, when he thus spoke again:

    "The winter's blasts of snow and hail
    With wrath report the mournful tale,
    'Your Pipe is out.' Alas! 'tis true.
    That ancient bowl from which I drew
    Sweet incense to the Goddess' shrine,
    Who guards the fragrant Nicotine,
    My badge of power, known far and wide,
    Where e'er my nimble Reindeers glide,
    Has lost its charm; and noisy Fame,
    With boist'rous shouts, I hear proclaim
    The praises of a rising star,
    I think you call its name—Cigar."

"Most benevolent sir, now the subject you mention,—
The ecstatic cigar,—I sincerely rejoice
For this chance to invite your most kindly attention
To my wants. For next Christmas a gen'rous invoice
Of Cheroots, this delightful and modern invention,
Is my earnest request and unalt'rable choice.
You'll be angry, I fear, but it's not overstated,
When I say your old Pipe has become antiquated.
The new God, the Cigar, its old realm has invested,
And his power firm established, he reigns unmolested.

    "But here, most ancient sir, to lay aside
    All metaphor, I'm willing to abide
    Your own opinion candidly expressed,
    First giving this cigar an honest test.

"And besides, *entre nous*, when you don't have to buy it,
I remark that its virtue is greater: Here,—try it."
In one hand I extended a box to his sight
Of Antiguedad firsts, in the other a light.

With slow and hesitating hand
He chooses, and assays the brand.
I see his twinkling eyes confess
The fragrant argument's success.
His fears forsake his troubled soul,
Breathed on the clouds that round him roll.
"I see my error now," he said,
"I've been a grumbler, and instead
Of watching innovation's pace,
To guard my laurels in the race,
Your modern enterprise I find
Has left me struggling far behind.
This truth no longer now concealed,
In yonder cloud I see revealed:
To all who yearly wait me here,
I'm still as welcome and as dear;
But yet, all efforts were in vain,
My wonted empire to retain,
Unless with zealous care I sought
Appropriate gifts for modern thought.

'My Pipe is out'! You say aright,
But from its ashes springs a light
That indicates the certain way
By which I can confirm my sway.
Old fogy notions here I'll throw aside,
And haste to overtake th' advancing stride
Of Progress. But, good night! I hear
Th' impatient pawing of my Deer.
'Tis many leagues of flight before
They'll see their distant stable's door.
Their breakfast waits them, and I fear
To keep them longer fretting here.
I'm off; but first I'll take a mem.
Concerning you next year.—Ahem!
I beg your pardon,—but I would suggest,
My journey will be long before I rest,—
Excuse me,—but the distance is so far,
I'll beg th' indulgence of a fresh cigar."

"Help yourself my old friend, there are plenty to spare,
It were shameful besides to refuse you a share."
I replenished his pouch with the solacing weeds,
While he loosened the reins of his beautiful steeds.
With a shout he was off, and a clatter and jingle,
Brought an end to my visit with jolly Kris Kringle.

www.ingramcontent.com/pod-product-compliance
Lightning Source LLC
Chambersburg PA
CBHW021834230426
43669CB00008B/965